What The Experts Are Saying

This book is a fascinating, comprehensive, revealing array of information and concepts about workforce training and education. Luskin clearly explains significant implications for a future where the Internet, media and new learning psychologies are playing an increasingly larger role. *Casting the Net Over Global Learning* is essential for any up to date eLearning library and essential for those studying media communication, media psychology and education leadership.

Dr. Judith Kuipers
President, Fielding Graduate Institute

Luskin provides a remarkably astute overview, with key new information, of how strategic changes in media, corporate education, and new knowledge about learning are altering global learning. I recommend it.

Dr. Kenneth (Casey) Green
Visiting Professor, Claremont Graduate University
Founder and Publisher, Campus Computing Report

Bernie Luskin is globally recognized as a major pioneer in media and education. His contributions are recognized milestones of accomplishment. This book represents another significant contribution to twenty first century literature in education and training. *Casting the Net Over Global Learning* is must reading for every education and media professional.

John Barker
Chairman, DVD Summit Conferences
Publisher, Inside Multimedia and DVDeye

Luskin captures new trends in executive development, including identifying and describing new key roles in corporate education and all of eLearning. Bernie Luskin is a true and articulate leader, and genuine pioneer in distributed education, learning psychology and media.

Dr. Ira Krinsky
Managing Partner, Korn Ferry International

What we learn depends on the experience we bring to the learning. Bernie Luskin brings a lifetime of success and experience to the world of distanced learning, media and communication. This book is a clear and thorough sharing of his valuable experience.

William Gladstone
Chairman (emeritus), GlobalLearningSystems
Publisher, Waterside Publishing

Casting the Net Over Global Learning significantly widens our optic and deepens our consciousness about the emergence of new corporate universities. Using new media, the new corporate university will have the effect that Gutenberg had on the Bible, Ford had on mass production, Einstein had on atomic energy and Gates is having on training. The new corporate university can be global and local, scholarly and professional, pedagogical and andragogical. It represents both traditional needs and futuristic methods. Luskin captures it all as he describes this multidimensional new phenomenon clearly, with clarity and cogency. This book is must reading for education and training professionals, and a key addition in every library.

Dr. Lenneal Henderson
Professor, University of Baltimore

Luskin defines the new leadership roles in the future of education and training. This is a must book for professionals.

Stephen Unger
Managing Partner, Media and Entertainment
Heidrick and Struggles

I have been deeply involved with the Internet and learning since its infancy. This book provides fresh insights about what drives the new global learning world, and most importantly, where it is going.

Dr. David Lavielle
Chief Policy Analyst for Education
California Post Secondary Education Commission

Bernie Luskin has transitioned media psychology and media communications as an education and training initiative in the world corporate and education community. Partnerships with Universities and Community Colleges will lead to new programs in Organizational Development, Media Studies, Communication, eLearning and Education Leadership and Change. It is a key resource.

Dr. Judy Witt
Dean, School of Education Leadership and Change
Fielding Graduate University

Technology is the syringe, psychology is the serum and they combine together to form and deliver the new media and learning opportunities in distributed education. Luskin is a pioneer in media psychology. He is leading the way in applying the principles of psychology to media in health care, government, entertainment, commerce and education. This book contains much new information.

Dr. Ronald Giannetti
Dean, School of Psychology
Fielding Graduate Institute

Casting the Net Over Global Learning is for all professionals who stay up to date in education, training and development, web-based education, performance management and improvement, executive education, leadership, corporate learning, organizational development, knowledge management, instructional design, College/University administration, human resources, corporate universities, media communication and media studies.

Dr. Joel Greenberg
Director of Strategic Development, British Open University

Community Colleges are central to the competitive future of the world and a cornerstone of the American economy. Bernie Luskin has been a community college, university, and corporate leader for more than a quarter century. He truly casts a net over global learning in a way that is understandable and relevant for the coming decade. This book and his new programs in Media Studies and Community College Leadership and Change at the Fielding Graduate Institute are pacesetters for this new century.

Ray Taylor
President and CEO, American Association of Community College Trustees

Bernie Luskin defines new partnership and alliance opportunities for community colleges. *Casting the 'Net* is a blueprint for partnerships. It is important reading for all community college leaders.

Dr. George Boggs
President and CEO, American Association of Community Colleges

Casting The Net over Global Learning

DR. BERNARD J. LUSKIN

Griffin Publishing Group
Irvine, California

Director of Operations:	Robin L. Howland
Project Manager:	Bryan Howland
Editor:	Toni T. Luskin
Editorial Assistance:	People Speak
Co-Author:	Toni T. Luskin
Contributors:	Peter Goldschmidt
	John Hoover
	Scott Sobel
Cover Design:	FirstPublish
Book Design:	m2designgroup

Griffin Publishing Group
18022 Cowan, Suite 202
Irvine, CA 92614
www.griffinpublishing.com

ISBN:1-58000-106-8
10 9 8 7 6 5 4 3 2 1

Dr. Luskin may be contacted at bjluskin@cs.com

Manufactured in the United States of America

Dedication

Casting the Net Over Global Learning is for those who wish to:

- Know the way,
- Show the way, and
- ·Go the way.

And is dedicated to:

- Esther and Morrie, my loving parents who showed me the way,
- Ryan and Matteo, our sons, whom we hope will go the way, and to
- Toni, my wife and co-author, who continually brings the breath of life, love, and purpose, and who always knows the way.

Bernard Luskin
Encino, California
2002

Table of Contents

Introduction

Secrets of Success: Implementing Global Learning in the Communications Age

In the past decade, there has been as much progress in learning psychology as in digital media, medicine, or biotechnology. Progress in using what we now know about learning and, especially the use of media in learning, has been slow. *Casting the Net Over Global Learning* is about what is happening now to provide a basis for executives, trainers, investors, administrators and learners to make intelligent choices for their futures. *Casting the Net Over Global Learning* examines:

- How human capital is replacing physical capital.

- How education is the difference between corporate success and failure.

- How the education and training industry is using new knowledge in psychology and advances in digital media in meeting the growing education challenge.

This book examines corporate, higher, adult, and K–12 education. It amplifies and explains key trends central to the comprehensive global development of new dimensions in workforce training, corporate education, and e-learning. This book will teach you:

- The ways in which knowledge and communications are changing competition.

- How to develop strategic education and training programs.

- How to apply emerging theories of learning to media.

Each chapter heading is self-explanatory and each chapter may be read individually. You will gain an overview of the content by reviewing the chapter headings.

It is not the strongest species that survive, nor the most intelligent, but the most responsive to change

— Charles Darwin

Chapter 1: Shaping Global Learning: Everything Changes Everything

This chapter identifies a series of *drivers* creating the trends that are changing the world of education and training. The material centers on the Internet, but addresses concerns about globalization and cultural dissonance, including the implications of September 11, 2001, and the future of global learning. Covered are a variety of forces converging to change education and training.

Chapter 2: The Emerging Corporate University

This chapter examines the growing global corporate university trend which has increasing impact on corporate education and training. It explains the metaphor and strategic contribution of the corporate university. The chapter examines the nature and form of the corporate university as an emerging segment of the recognized educational establishment. It provides support for the contention that corporate education and training will be a competitive differentiator in this century.

Chapter 3: Examples of Corporate Universities

Information on the emergence of the corporate university as a metaphor and structure for corporate education and training is provided in this chapter. This chapter specifically identifies a cross section of different types of corporate universities and provides detail to aid the reader to follow up on each.

Chapter 4: Hail to the Chiefs

This chapter explains the emerging "Chiefs" and their career identities and roles. The job of the CLO (Chief Learning Officer) is explained, as well as the trends toward creating other chiefs' positions including the CPO (Chief People Officer), CKO (Chief Knowledge Officer), CIO (Chief Information Officer), CEO (Chief Executive Officer), CFO (Chief Financial Officer), and the growing popularity of the Solutions Architect in developing and addressing your company's learning needs. The elevated status of knowledge workers in the corporate market place is also analyzed. Specific descriptions of the new positions are provided. The increasing importance of these roles is underlined.

Chapter 5: Ivy-Covered Clicks

This chapter addresses the significant growth of distance education in colleges and universities. It examines higher education developments and provides examples.

Chapter 6: If I Only Had a Brain

Learning is a function of diverse factors. This chapter describes the physical aspects of the brain in learning and relates the physical brain to learning and media. It explains the extraordinary advances in understanding the physical and theoretical dimensions of learning *and* learning theory and the importance of understanding both the physical and theoretical frameworks to learning. It recognizes that in today's world it is imperative to understand both the physical brain plus the theories, strategies, and techniques which enable learning.

Chapter 7: Learning Theories

This chapter presents an overview of key e-learning theories and reviews the theoretical aspects of learning as they relate to emerging new media. Theories addressed include the nature of perception and reality, theories of attention, positive addiction, believability and the suspension of disbelief, forced feedback techniques, the implications of color, graphics and sound, semiotics; including the importance of iconography and navigation, semantics, synesthetics, learning and motivation, retention, psycho visualization, memory; both long and short term, mastery, literacy, trying, learned helplessness, and theories of success.

Chapter 8: The Psychologies of Producing Media

Specific psychologies related to various aspects of media communications and online learning are presented. Included is an examination of the nature and requirements of production, editing media, and the relationships between the theories studied and their application in actual production.

Chapter 9: K–12, The Learning Continuum, Work, and the 'Net

This chapter explains and emphasizes the importance of kindergarten through life-long learning and highlights the research substantiating the importance of early learning for future intellectual, emotional, and social growth. It also provides new support for the premise that early learning is a key to developing basic skills for the workforce of the future.

Chapter 10: Choosing the Way Ahead

The deficit between the steep ascent of advancing technology and the flatter ascent of human learning is called the "skills gap." *Casting the 'Net Over Global Learning* presents the "how to" for closing the gap. Here we take a look into the future in the context of the dramatically shifting environment over the past several years.

Casting the 'Net Over Global Learning is for:

a. Corporate executives who need to stay competitive in the new Information Age.

b. Corporate trainers who need to close the skills gap in the workforce.

c. Educators who need to educate and graduate employable students.

d. Administrators (at all levels) who currently work in two- and four-year public, private, and for-profit colleges and universities.

e. Graduate students interested in the impact of information technology and media on the postsecondary institutions.

f. Corporate and educational executives who need to stay competitive in the new Communications Age.

g. Educators interested in Media Studies and eMedia in learning.

h. Practitioners evolving their fundamental knowledge of media centric learning.

i. Professionals in education, commerce, health care, entertainment, and publishing who are interested in understanding electronic learning, media, and in charting the way ahead.

j. Individuals exploring new career opportunities in the education and training arenas.

Summary

The book cuts across all sectors of education (e.g., two- and four-year colleges and universities, corporate and workforce education and training, and K–12.The education community has long had great aspirations and high expectations for the role of technology and media in teaching, learning, and instruction. These aspirations, initially fostered by radio and then film in the first half of the 20th century, grew dramatically with the arrival of television in the 1950s, mainframe computers and cable in the 1960s, and more recently, the enabling technologies represented by the satellite networks and the personal computer in the 1980s and the Internet and the Web in the past decade. Together, these technologies represent stunning improvement in media and communications. Indeed, the evolving Internet/ post-dot.com economy offers a unique opportunity to assess the impact of information technology and media on instruction, teaching, institutional planning and policy in postsecondary institutions and in corporate training.

This book explores the impact of a wide range of information and telecommunications technologies, media, and new applications of theories and psychologies to teaching and learning in higher/post-secondary environments and in corporate education. In the book I cover the landscape as we explore the great expectations as well as real benefits and outcomes for the role of information, media and communications technology in education.

Comments or questions may be directed to the author at bjluskin@cs.com

Author's Notes

I wish to thank Bob Howland, president of Griffin Publishing Group, for his help and encouragement and making the publication of this book a reality. Thanks to Bryan and Robin Howland for their help in getting the manuscript ready. My wife, Toni, has my gratitude for her many contributions to this book as contributor and editor and for facilitating life. Also, special thanks to Peter Goldschmidt, who was always concerned, helpful, and full of good advice. Finally, my thanks to my mother, Esther Luskin, age eighty-nine at the time of this writing, who has recently conquered the mystery of sending email.

Preface

e-Learning is emerging from the convergence of media, the web and growth in understanding the true nature of learning on all levels. There is growth on all fronts. These include K–12, college, or business, and embrace workforce training and media communication writ large. In the world of competition, applied knowledge is now recognized as fundamental and key to a company's competitive advantage and is acknowledged as a key human capitol asset. The forces developing e-Learning are stimulating corporate development across the world. The investor community continues to be positively supportive of new learning initiatives.

Media centric and e-Learning, including web-based or online learning is likely to be the fastest-growing method for creating access to education and training in the next quarter century. Megatrends in areas such as understanding literacy, brain based learning, population demographics, technology, globalization, branding, consolidation, privatization, and outsourcing will greatly affect the way we approach learning. Professionals and practititioners need to understand each of these trends to be effective in what they do.

These megatrends are affecting all learning markets. The segments are early education, K–12 education, post-secondary education, corporate training, and we must include consumer products and services. The increasing need for skilled labor in the commercial world will continually increase the need for e-Learning. Many of the breakthroughs in learning strategies will now come from online e-manuals and websites, fast replacing the paper instruction book previously sold with products. This trend will be central to advances in learning technique because it is based on competition and will be a must for the success of any product.

The astounding growth of the Internet is increasing its continuing impact. In the next three years, devices connecting to the wired and wireless Internet will number in the hundreds of millions. In the four-year period between 1998 and 2002, 300 million new global users came online. Global online advertising spending will soon reach $50 billion in 2005. e-Commerce will top the $1 trillion mark in 2003. AOL, Yahoo, Microsoft, IBM, AT&T, Sun Microsystems, Oracle, Harcourt, Sylvan, McGraw Hill, Pearson, Philips, Sony, Matshushita, Thomson, Newscorp, are only examples of companies pushing the envelope.

The global education and training market is a $2 trillion industry, with $750 billion in the U.S. Approximately 10% of the $750 billion is "for-profit" business. In the corporate sector, media centric and classroom and on-line variations on e-Learning are changing classroom training which includes a great deal of sophisticated media strategies, new blending with the internet, including online variations and over the next few years will be pervasive in the overall workforce training market. Additional trends include home schooling, which is growing at 15% per year and will soon be a billion dollar market of its own. In the lifelong learner market, self-help books grew at a 20% plus rate from 1993-1997, and in addition, 90% of people that go online also do so to pursue information about a hobby or lifelong interest. This is a natural byproduct of the growing assimilation of the Internet as a central ingredient of normal life. This personal interest aspect of the market is growing and companies such as Digital Directions International, on whose board I serve, is leading the way (PrivateLessons.net) through its partner network with PBS and AOL.

As this book goes to publication, America and the world are pulling out of a recessionary slump. The new investor class, i.e., those 30-50, who are suburban homeowners, highly educated, and likely to invest are licking their wounds caused by the 2001 dot.bombs, the 911 terrorism attacks, and the post-Enron, Global Crossing disillusionment, all of which cost the group over 35 more than thirty percent of their accumulated wealth. During 2002, then, these investors became angry, disillusioned and felt betrayed and are now pulling themselves together and moving to the new future.

The reality check is now taking us forward. We are moving from a world where disbelief was suspended, to a world based on more common sense. I believe it will be a world of great opportunity for those who recognize that opportunity. To quote Winston Churchill,

> *The pessimist sees the difficulty in every opportunity.*
> *The optimist sees the opportunity in every difficulty.*

Education and training will give companies the needed competitive advantage in the next quarter century. The emerging human and organizational structures which will facilitate this advantage include the emergence of the corporate university as a vehicle for workforce training, the increasing sophistication of the learning and training leadership personified in the coming of the Chiefs, and the tremendous advances in media and learning psychology, i.e., the realization that technology is the syringe and psychology is the serum. Blend them together in new and sophisticated ways and you have global e-commerce driven by eMedia Communication, and a media centric workforce-learning environment that will be cast like a net over Global Learning. This is the subject I will address in depth throughout this book. This embraces the new fields of knowledge that the scholar/practitioners of the new century will learn and apply and which will set this group apart among the new leadership of the 21st century.

Bernard J. Luskin
Encino, California
March 2002

Shaping
Global Learning:
Everything Changes Everything

It has become common to hear that, "the Internet is changing everything." However, to be more accurate and complete, in today's world, "everything is changing everything." With respect to technology, the Web obviously changes a great deal. Digital technology, advances in DVD technology, including "Learning on the go" through PDA's and other emerging devices, internal computer digital processing speeds and capacities, and wireless technologies continue to rapidly alter the concept of the Web and the nature and context of global communications. Wired and wireless advances will change the concept of what we now think of as the Internet and the net that is being cast over global learning.

The many advances in telecommunications are revolutionizing the technical and behavioral nature of communications. Broad global initiatives, including many corporate mergers and acquisitions, are now creating truly linked global workforces, serving worldwide markets that

The Internet is changing social class and boundaries. One of the latest wrinkles is the narrowing divide between teachers and learners.

— John Makulowich, U.S.A. Today

are changing the nature of competition. Multinational companies are spawning entirely new sets of strategies for addressing the diverse needs in corporate education and training. Technology has changed how we think about and use geography. With the "death of distance," the need for common learning and common understanding is here.

With the concept of the Web changing and evolving, pundits are stumped as to what modalities will look like twenty years from now. The way we watch television, listen to radio, read and publish books and newspapers, and use computers and personal devices is changing. Personal preference networks in health, food, private lessons, discovery, and sports (from football to equestrian) programming have emerged. More than ever before, viewers follow their own interests in choosing what to watch. In addition, personal preference, "living cable" networks and many personal preference books and newspapers are now online, and print-on-demand, speech recognition, and new PCPDATV combinations are already on the market. Moreover, the nature of the print on demand, speech recognition and PCPDA combinations is rapidly advancing in each case.

The expanding freedom of choice in education, information, and entertainment is altering how we spend our time. Whereas we once crowded around the TV set to watch a program on one of the major networks, we now scan through hundreds of cable and satellite channels or migrate to the computer or Web-enabled devices that combine TV and the 'Net. New double-screen, split-screen, TV PC and PCTV styles of use are emerging. Companies like ClickVision, Tivo, Vidyah, and Imerge are only a few examples of companies introducing new TV interface strategies. Dan Bates, CEO of Creative Frontier, Inc., has developed Click Vision as an embedded interface that may be used on any PC or TV system.

Simply put, boundaries are disappearing. The future is blended, and it is screen deep in entertainment, education, and workforce training. Screen deep implying that all devices will converge in various forms. Information on most subjects can now be found on the Web, which means that in a sense, the Internet has become an information extension to normal, intelligent functioning. Today, it is common to be fascile with search engines, encyclopedic and e-communications features of the Internet. What is as yet uncommon is the sophisticated use of pictures, graphics, and sounds that exploit the dynamic sensory and emotional power of many programs. This area will be the next wave of development and the historically passive, "lean back" behaviors of television viewing will now converge with the "lean forward" behaviors of computer use.

The average time spent on the Web by Internet users in the Unites States in October 2000 was ten hours and four minutes per week. This compared to eight hours and thirteen minutes reported in October 1999. During that same period, Web page views per person jumped from 524 pages per month to 720 pages per month. Overall, America's one-hundred million Internet users are spending more and more time using Internet services and resources.

What a Tangled Web...

As noted earlier, definitions of the Web are changing and new devices, both wired and wireless, are proliferating. The best way to fully appreciate the scope and dimension of what is evolving is to examine trends to establish a foundation for understanding the direction in which the convergence of wired and wireless devices and the media psychologies are evolving.

Some Perspective

In 1999 there were 800 million pages on the World Wide Web, yet it is interesting to note that even the best search engine at that time could access only about 16 percent, or 128 million of them. Today the most comprehensive single search you may mount will still miss about 84 percent, or 672 million pages. How many of those pages on the Web have anything to do with the topic you're researching? It is clear that Web opportunity and access has grown dramatically, yet in reality, we are only beginning to have access to all we want to find. What is useful to understand here is that the magnitude of information is increasing rapidly, yet search methods are still rudimentary in terms of what they will become in years ahead. I believe that the speed and accuracy of searches will continue to increase quickly.

The sheer volume of data and information sources on the Internet has given rise to enterprises like Open Channel at the University of Chicago. Open Channel markets *"open-source"* software. Roughly translated, open-source software is software that is readily available and accessible at no cost. So how can Open Channel charge money for Website delivery of something that's already free? Issues of cost and access are the fundamental factors of growing global use.

One way that Open Channel and similar enterprises add value to the universe of free software is by organizing it. Obviously, it does not matter how much information is available on the Web if you cannot find it. Open Channel organizes software by discipline, mostly for use in academic settings. Many software programs that are valuable but too small or narrowly focused to enjoy widespread appeal are available, but are floating in an ocean of more frequently used software with much broader reach. Open channel is an example of an access strategy. The point here is that many times access is more important than distribution. A great deal of valuable information may be available—but not accessible. Choice, options, access, and diversity are the key features of future personal use of the Internet.

The Wave

One major trend to be aware of regarding the web is growth both in networks and data. The reason is simple: digital technology has changed the way we now live and do business. Think about the changes. Do you make phone calls? Do you drive a car? Do you adjust the thermostat in your home? Do you use an automatic teller machine to do some or all of your banking? Do you ever buy a soft drink or a candy bar from a machine? Every time you do one of these or a thousand other tasks, from the simple to the complicated, you are operating a computer. Interestingly, the largest manufactures and users of computers are automobile manufactures. The single largest user of computers in the United States is General Motors.

As global connectivity and technological capability and capacity expand, the most ordinary activities such as cooking and watching television are becoming microprocessor driven to the point that the average person may soon need to be micro-processor literate to carry out everyday ordinary tasks. For those who have yet to master the programming of their VCR, the tidal wave of technological innovation and progress sweeping over us is, at best, mildly unsettling to many. However, simplicity of design, advances in remotes and controllers, including understanding symbols (semiotics) on these devices has created a new global language in communication, easing the way in the emerging simple to use world of devices between continents and cultures. Semiotics, i.e., the development, manipulation, and use of symbols, is part of the new global language of iconography that we will examine in more detail later.

According to International Data Corporation (IDC) the global population of Web users 1998 totaled 142 million. One year later that number had grown to 196 million, with 100 million of those users being adults in the United States. IDC projects that there will be more than 500 million Internet users around the world by the end of 2003. The trend is clear.

The exceptional growth in Internet users is less likely a result of how much fun it is to surf the Web as much as it is a result of how vital Web activity has become to doing business, both personal and professional, or learning or gathering information. Mediamark Research reports that adult men and women use the Web in approximately equal numbers. The fastest growing segment of computer users is senior citizens and the fastest growing segments of the active Web population are adolescents and preadolescents. Online activity will increasingly eclipse more traditional forms of global communications. (One example of this can be seen in the preferences toward e-mail after the anthrax mail episodes in fall 2001).

Swiss Army Controller

Three Dimensional Chess

In addition to allowing reciprocal transmission of data, the Internet performs multiple tasks allowing for the exchange of video (continually improving), audio, text, and graphics. Along with access to millions of Web sites and vast libraries of information user can also have a cyber conversation with others around the globe. The Internet allows microprocessors to function on a concept akin to a cyber Swiss Army knife by facilitating choice, options, access, diversity, creativity, and personal preference.

You can navigate forward, backward, side-to-side, up and down… anywhere you want to go…anytime. The sheer complexity of the Web can be intimidating and, for some, immobilizing. Whatever your problem, the solution you are looking for can, more than likely, be found somewhere on the Web. It sounds simple, but is it easy to find and implement meaningful solutions to the challenges facing your organization?

When we talk about all the things that can be done with the Internet as a tool, we must realize that it is just that— a tool. Despite all of its wonders, one of the realities of the web is that it is presently, simply a largely underused tool. If your experience with the Internet to this point has not delivered the results you want, our advice is to think in a new dimension, which is the real purpose of this description.

Size Matters

The Dean of the University of California at Berkeley's School of Information Management, Hal Varian, and Professor Peter Lyman, as a result of their research conclude that the Internet is flooding us with information — and the tide is rising. Varian and Lyman noted that increasing computer power, falling digital storage prices and, most of all, the rise of the Net are all contributing to the staggering amount of information that is being disseminated daily around the world via radio, television, and computers, and then stored digitally or magnetically.

The U.C. Berkeley study measured the amount of "unique information" generated each year worldwide at one and one-half exabytes. An exabyte is a *one* followed by 18 zeros. If one and one-half exabytes were stored on floppy discs, the stack of discs would be 2 million miles high. If you distribute one and one-half exabytes of information equally among every man, woman, and child on earth, each individual would be given the equivalent of 250 books or floppy discs. Varian and Lyman went on to report that 93 percent of the information produced each year is stored digitally.

According to the study, amount of e-mail sent by individuals is *500 times greater* than the total number of Web pages. At the time the study was released, there were over 2 billion static pages on the Web. Just think about the amount of information in the Library of Congress alone. David Shenk, author of *Data Smog: Surviving the Information Glut*, says, "It's no longer a question of access to information, but the challenge of weeding through to find what you need." As noted earlier, one of the fundamental concepts in Web economics is "access."

The Internet is growing exponentially. Individuals will only encounter portions of it in their lifetimes. For some it will primarily be a source of entertainment and amusement. Others will shop for everything from beer to beds and automobiles to airplanes. Many will conduct all of their financial activates online. More and more business is conducted on the Web every day and more and more businesses are becoming almost completely virtual. Interestingly, it is my observation that growing numbers of people use the Web as a primary mode of communications with friends and family.

Social Architecture

Among the many changes the Internet is bringing to our lives, perhaps the most profound are the ways in which it affects society. The National Research Council (NRC) recently published a study in 2000 which states that "large-scale information systems are as much social systems as they are systems for organizing information". The report called for additional research funding to study how well expanding information technology is meeting society's needs. The NRC concluded that large-scale socio-technical systems and the methods for designing such systems lack sufficient funding. That is another way of articulating that many aspects of the Internet are poorly designed at this stage. Also addressing concerns about the ways in which media and technology affect individuals and society are two emerging fields of study: media psychology and media literacy. These rapidly growing disciplines concentrate on profound questions such as: What are the ways in which new media and new technologies impact behavior? What is the changing and expanding definition(s) of literacy in the early twenty-first century?

It is not surprising that the implications of the Internet's effect upon social issues are poorly defined at this stage of technological development. As highlighted, the Internet, new media, and the telecommunications technology that drives it, are evolving faster than we can analyze them. The rapid evolution and expansion of the Internet, along with the revolutionary changes in communication technology and connectivity have simply outpaced our current abilities to conduct rigorous research and inquiry and to validate their conclusions. A pitfall of current research design is that it is frequently tainted by assumptions based on past paradigms and past practice. The material you are reading has been written to provoke new thoughts about concepts for research design and other new factors to help us plan the way ahead.

A paradigm shift in communication practices has begun. Examples of rapid changes in the business sector are e-billing systems and the conduct of online learning and commerce of any type. While e-mail has changed communication significantly, most billing has remained in the domain of regular mail. Responses, such as payments and correspondence, have been paper-centric in much the same way they have been for the past two centuries. Many large companies have launched customer campaigns to encourage bill paying by alternative methods such as direct debit from checking accounts and various pay-by-phone or online options. The changes now will be dramatic. Reports, letters, correspondence, and especially bills, will become more and more electronic as the United States and other countries increase measures to counteract the possibility of bioterrorism attacks on traditional mail services. Companies will move, almost frantically, away from traditional practice. World events have created a resurgence in the momentum toward developing advanced communications technologies.

In the past, most inventions requiring scrutiny have remained stable long enough to allow for observation, experimentation, and understanding. Television's mass introduction into American society in the 1950's *seemed* to arrive with a bang. The same could be said for the introduction of radio and the telephone earlier in the same century. But, all of these phenomena actually settled in and grew slowly by today's standards — and those new technologies didn't change radically month-to-month and year-to-year. Media observers and philosophers of the first half of the twentieth century had more time to formulate and argue their theories of the various technologies' impact on society and, culture. More recently, studies such as those done by Media Scope and the Academy of Television Arts and Sciences, have been conducted to see how televised violence affects juvenile behavior and how television viewing affects academic performance. Those findings were, and still are, debated, analyzed, and reanalyzed. However, this research does have two conclusions that are widely accepted in some quarters: Exposure to violence can desensitize one to violence and exposure to violence can cause violence.

Using old-fashioned study methods to examine the Internet, new media, and new technologies will more than likely produce immediately outdated findings. The velocity of progress and change within the areas being studied will out pace our ability to conduct serious research using current methodology. Certainly, we should neither neglect nor abandon the understanding and guidance that research brings to our decision-making. We must go far beyond the conclusions of the National Research Council. Should media research be better funded? Absolutely. We must, however, develop enhanced research methodologies that take into account the ever-changing nature of media and communications. New career opportunities for solutions architects, knowledge officers, information officers, and learning officers will emerge along with new fields of study such as media literacy and media psychology.

Isolation or Inclusion?

One of the questions plaguing media watchers is whether or not new media, the Internet, and the Web promote social isolation or social integration. Those arguing that isolation is the trend cite the fact that e-mail often takes the place of walking down the hall at the office and knocking on a colleague's door. In a larger sense, the increasing number of individuals who work from home, thanks to Internet and intranet capabilities, have progressively less and less social interaction than they formerly experienced in the workplace. Traditional team-building techniques now must be radically altered to accommodate virtual work teams that rarely meet face to face, either because of the participants' telecommuting or vast geographical distances. Research indicates that people who have met face to face work more easily together using the Internet than those who have not met in person because a relationship is established and that makes electronic communication feel like a simple, easy, and effective way to stay in touch.

Studies conducted by Stanford University and the Free University of Berlin (among others) assert that too much time spent on the Internet makes some people reclusive and less likely to interact with others in person. In another study released in 2000 researchers arrived at a different conclusion. A study financed by the Pew Foundation involved a sample of 3,533 adults who appear to be closer to friends and loved ones thanks to the Internet and Web.

A total of 55 percent of the respondents in the Pew Foundation study stated that they actually improved communications with family, and 66 percent reported increased contact with friends via the Web. However, the study also found that most e-mail users still prefer snail mail or the telephone when discussing upsetting or troublesome topics with others they don't see in person. While the majority of Web users studied increased their contact with friends and relatives, those same users didn't feel as if the Web necessarily brought them emotionally and/or relationally closer to others. This remains a debate and an interesting area where research will lead to greater understanding. Also, people tend to answer e-mail with e-mail, telephone calls with telephone calls, and letters with letters. Once individuals consciously recognize that e-mail may precipitate a telephone response, the comfort level and effectiveness of various modes of communication will improve.

In the Pew study, most respondents used the Internet more as a research tool than as a tool for interpersonal communications. In addition, women surveyed were most likely to seek information on health, religion, new jobs, or to play games online. The men in the study were most likely to seek out news, sports, financial information, and to shop online. It appears that women and men are using the Internet to do things that telephones, radios, and one-way television don't do as well as interconnected communications, and this is an intriguing trend to ponder. Interestingly, the research for the Pew study was conducted using *telephone interviews.*

Whereas the general population is still divided between Internet users and non-users, it seems like most individuals studied preferred using the telephone. Again, psychologists studying the assimilation of the evidence argue that mixed response will be the effective way of the future. Answering an e-mail with a telephone call is a sign of overcoming rigidity in the communication process. Moreover, the old telephone paradigm is also shifting. The omnipresent telephone is the nexus of a new media product show. Dominant multi-national communication companies like AT&T, Time Warner, MCI WorldCom, and Direct TV are now leveraging our old friend, the telephone, as an intrinsic part of a total, one-stop-shopping communications package. On the horizon is the one-device-fits-all opportunity.

Convergent technologies are now experiencing explosive growth. Witness technologies such as voice- over-cable and satellite and cable morphed communications (so-called fixed cable, where signals are beamed to small pizza-sized dishes affixed outside homes to disseminate telephony/video/Internet signals to stations within the house). As communication lines and models change, so will the comfort levels we have with using the new tools as truly personal communicators. The future winners in the trendy communications landscape will be those who know how to best use the new mediums. Wireless communications, personal digital assistants, infrared links, and all manner of digital advances are now bringing even more dramatic changes and the new PDAs are merging them together.

Trusting Trends

Understanding communication in action is the challenge. The Pew Foundation study provides diverse data and analysis to ponder while it underscores the importance of understanding communications in action.

Many innovations are transcendent and their successes fragile. The people who brought us Federal Express were enjoying the financial fruits of their tremendously successful new enterprise when they apparently detected that the rapid delivery of documents was becoming a trend. Federal Express moved quickly and caught the United States Postal Service and United Parcel Service by surprise. While USPS and UPS were still scrambling along with others to get up to speed in the overnight delivery business, the top minds at FedEx were cooking up even *faster* ways to deliver documents.

For a sizable fee, FedEx would pick up your document(s) and transmit them via satellite to the destination city, where a company employee would promptly deliver them to the recipient. The whole process took about an hour. It was another revolutionary idea that seemed like the natural next step in the overnight delivery concept. However, FedEx executives who were sharing in the profits of their already booming business envisioned those profits being diverted toward the expensive, continuing development of the Zap Mail system, which also included some development of satellite technology.

In the 1980s, Zap Mail also had a challenger looming on the horizon. Facsimile machines cost about the same as several Zap Mail deliveries and *fax machines* could do in minutes what Zap Mail took an hour or more to do. The trend seemed clear enough, and the executives at FedEx recognized it. What even they did not count on was the rapidity of the evolving technology. In the case of the facsimile machine, availability and affordability brought about widespread market penetration and common use faster than anyone could have imagined. Zap Mail got zapped.

In light of recent developments in national security, the United States Postal Service will no doubt revolutionize its complete communications strategy. The changes will most likely be beyond any that we can presently imagine.

Worldwide Web

One illustration of how the Internet surmounts many of the obstacles to globalization in graduate education is the University of Phoenix. The University of Phoenix is the largest private university in the United States and it continues to expand across the country. Responding to increased demand for education that focuses primarily on business studies, the University of Phoenix is developing, acquiring, and creating partnerships with learning institutions in several Latin American countries, Europe, China, India, and Mexico. The Internet provides the digital yarn that knits them all together.

Globalization of the Workforce

This trend is clear. Customers are everywhere. Employees are winding up everywhere. Multinational airline partnerships like American Airlines One World program are a direct reflection of how national boundaries are being smudged, and sometimes erased altogether, by corporate mergers, acquisitions, and alliances. Dealing with these new geographical and cultural challenges is serious business. Thomas L. Friedman put it like this:

Globalization isn't a choice. It's a reality. There is just one global market today, and the only way you can grow at the speed [you] want to grow is to tap into the global stock and bond markets, by seeking out multinationals to invest in your company, and by selling into the global trading system.

The 24/7 flexibility of e-learning easily spans time zones. Local languages are becoming an issue for course designers to consider, and so are local customs. The flexibility of e-learning can accommodate those types of specifics, but we must be aware of intercultural differences and intercultural dissonances. The context of our understanding of people must extend beyond borders and transcend cultures.

B2B

The Internet has opened a world of possibilities and opportunities in education, training, and learning. Companies are using digital communications as a competitive weapon. The Internet is an information management tool that enhances agility and responsiveness, reduces lead times, increases operating efficiency, and dramatically improves customer service and satisfaction. Companies are scrambling to get up to speed and stay up to speed with their employees' Internet skills just to stay competitive. Despite global economic ups and downs, we are moving toward a rebirth in telecommunications, education, and training. The "dot com" era of the late twentieth century seemed to be filled with young entrepreneurs of significant ability and little historical memory of the evolution of modern communications technologies. The new resurgence will be headed by many of those same entrepreneurs, now not quite so young, but with a perspective on where the new technologies have come from.

Companies now centralize and manage data in real time on enterprise resources spread throughout the globe. The procurement and production supply chain for millions of products is fully automated. Online marketplaces have produced new processes for consumers and suppliers alike. Thanks to the Internet, an item that hitherto sat and gathered dust in a second-hand store can now be auctioned off to the highest bidder from anywhere in the world.

The Internet has radically transformed practically every business. *U.S.A. Today* published a feature article on November 13, 2000, that cited a wide range of enterprises that have been transformed or made possible by the Internet. The list included a firm that has developed a method for decorating caskets with works of art or photographs.

The casket company's Website serves as a monthly catalog for funeral directors. The funeral directors can use the site to show models to customers and then place their order online. Executives at the casket company say that their business would have not been possible without the ubiquitous presence and immediacy of the Internet. Print catalogs and traditional ordering practices just can't support the volume of orders necessary to stay in business.

Wherever a computer is functioning, human beings have opportunities to piggyback other applications. Digital communications technology now makes it possible for people playing slot machines in a casino to make reservations at any of the resort's restaurants or tee times on the golf course on the slot machine they are playing. Organic farmers can put their produce on the Net for auction before the crop is harvested.

Movies Made for Television

Once upon a time, television was expected to empty out movie theaters and drive a stake through the heart of Hollywood. Nielsen Media Research tells us that people with Internet access at home watch 10 percent less TV than those in non-Net homes. In truth, Web activity is not replacing the television at all. It is preparing to merge with it, in much the same way that Hollywood now makes feature films that will eventually be sold for television distribution. The extended use or re-purposing of assets is a good strategy.

Television is being reborn. It is moving up a notch on the technology scale to realize more of its inherent potential. Cyber Dialogue estimates that more than thirty million Americans will access the Internet *via their TV sets* by 2006. In fact, as the computer and television set become increasingly synergetic and interactive, workforce education, using these new variations on common devices, will become more and more a part of the workday in the workplace, just as educational television has become part of the school day. ClickVision is a company that is developing the integrated one-screen, two-screen work of applications combining television with the Internet. CEO Dan Bates argues that the future portends a two-screen lean-forward world.

Showtime Networks Inc. and Paul Kagan Associates Inc. jointly published a report called "The Connected Household" in which they point out that *"In one quarter of all households nationwide—nearly 23 million—personal computers are in the same room as [television sets] and viewers in nearly 80 percent of those homes watch TV while surfing the Net."* In the report, *"TV/PC co-users"* in *"convergent households"* are referred to as *"multitasking viewers."* The future is screen deep, interactive and under user's control.

Mining the Mind

As we encounter communications technology in more and more aspects of our lives, the desire to understand the psychological and social implications will increase significantly. Figuring out the meaning of life is getting more complicated every day. The world of digital media is coming together like the pieces of an enormous puzzle.

It is interesting to remember that wealth was once mined from the earth in the form of oil, minerals, and precious metals. Now, and in the foreseeable future, the greatest fortunes will be "mined from the mind." The chapters ahead will describe how learning and new media come together, and how learning, work, competition, communications technology, globalization, and the new psychologies blend in the path ahead.

From Three R's to Three S's

In a world driven by knowledge, life-long learning has become the road to success. As the new knowledge and communication economies evolve, the traditional notion of literacy defined by the three R's (reading, writing, and 'rithmetic) is now changing and expanding to include what might be referred to as the three S's (synesthetics, semiotics, and semantics). Advancing synesthetics (feelings through our five senses), semiotics (the recognition and study of symbols), and semantics (words for communicating) are enabling the user experience.

The Future Belongs To Those Who Learn How To Learn

Today, the ability to navigate the Web can, and often does, develop prior to acquiring mastery of the three traditional R's. Adults who look condescendingly at kids playing warp speed-video games are missing several important points, not the least of which is that, in the world of business, standing still may be fatal. Most organizations that fall behind in the technology derby stand little chance of catching up, much less winning, in a rapidly changing marketplace. The future belongs to those who learn how to learn. In the world ahead, basic skills, new literacies, new media, and work will converge in new ways.

New Use for a New Tool

Potentially, the most profound use of the Internet is learning, (this includes pre-school, kindergarten through high school, undergraduate, post-graduate, and adult learning). The Internet promises, more than any other tool for erudition, to make learning for work and lifetime learning possible anywhere, anytime. The hottest ember in the online learning furnace is organizational learning for employed adults. "Learning is moving out of the training rooms and onto the Internet as corporations turn to e-learning to meet their needs for delivering effective learning."

Corporations need to involve increasingly decentralized employees, business partners, and customers dispersed around the globe in workforce training and education. Employees need access to learning solutions where they are and on the schedule that best suits them. The communication, storage, community-building, interactive, synchronous, and asynchronous aspects of the Internet make it the most flexible and scalable tool available to assist learning.

Boundaries Are Gone

The Internet is an expanse without boundaries. It offers infinite possibilities for enhancing human contact. An e-mail can deliver the simple instruction to pick up bread on the way home from work as well as a telephone call or an in-person chat can. Online communications also make it possible to compose and reflect on more sensitive messages before delivering them. Yet, the totality of the experience that takes place between two or more individuals who gather in person, i.e., their Gestalt, cannot be duplicated electronically…yet. It is the human dimension that brings the technology to life and all new media are simply tools to enhance human communications.

In *The Chronicle of Higher Education,* reporter Scott Carlson covered the startup of an online psychological counseling program. Noting that e-mail is not expected to replace the one-on-one session with a therapist, there are some aspects of therapy that psychologists are hoping to move permanently to an interactive psychology Web site. The site offers easy content, like a directory to local mental health resources, as well as more challenging crisis counseling that currently takes place mostly over telephone hotlines.

The psychology Website is expected to succeed for a variety of reasons. In part it is appealing because individuals in search of therapy, particularly young persons, are increasingly technology minded and computer-savvy. They are used to communicating online and, to varying degrees, may feel more comfortable sharing certain information from a distance. Among the challenges online counseling presents to the therapist is the ability to monitor the veracity of comments not made in the sanctity of a counseling room. There are, however times when complete anonymity brings out truths that certain individuals would never mention directly.

The current iteration of the psychology Website is designed to be used mostly for "pop" psychology topics such as health information, self-improvement, and non-critical relational issues. For *in-depth therapy,* clients will be referred back to local therapists for more conventional client/therapist relationships. However, the use and effectiveness of sites such as this will evolve in sophistication over time.

Therapists are presently trained to observe visual and auditory cues. University courses on Internet Psychotherapy are beginning to emerge. In addition, there are many seminars sponsored by various continuing education sources that focus on techniques for online interviewing and interventions. The field of psychology is adapting to the changing manner in which people communicate as well as other social adjustments brought on by technological advancements. It makes sense that psychologists and sociologists are paying increasing attention to the ways that digital technology and the Internet affect our lives. Information is power and money. Division 46, the Media Psychology Division, of the American Psychological Association is growing and diversifying. My own media program in the doctoral program at the Fielding Graduate Institute is attracting students who have ongoing careers in law, law enforcement, healthcare, human resources, information technology, education, and workforce training.

The Emerging Digital Divide

One real and disturbing trend of the technology boom is the emerging Digital Divide being brought about by the Internet. A significant political topic, the issues of possession of technology and *access* to the Web is a significant concern. We are all familiar to some degree with the widening economic gap, (the Digital Divide), between the *haves* and *have-lesses* in Western society.

Claremont Graduate University in Southern California is home to the Tomás Rivera Policy Institute. The Digital Steppingstones project at the Institute is funded by the W.K. Kellogg Foundation to identify challenges that must be addressed to develop and sustain programs that provide equal access to the Internet in low-income communities. Those who monitor social trends have observed that the information super-highway tends to bypass low-income and minority communities. Studies in Chicago, New York, Los Angeles, Houston, and Miami pointed to the need for more on-ramps to the information highway, particularly in disadvantaged areas.

Although the problem is not so complicated to identify, it is distinctly *more* complicated to remedy. The Digital Divide issue is part of the total economic paradigm. As hard as we try to work on the economics of poverty, it is a difficult situation to overcome. It takes money to purchase computers. It takes even more money to keep abreast of advances in computer technology. While many are free, it also takes money to subscribe to an Internet service provider. Earlier research by Claremont's Tomás Rivera Policy Institute found that across America, 80 percent of households earning less than $20,000 annually do not have home computers. But 80 percent of households with incomes of $75,000 or more do. Leaders like Roberta Weintraub, founder of High-tech High School, a public magnet school in the Los Angeles Unified School District, with the support of school district superintendents like Roy Romer, are at the forefront in addressing and solving these problems. With this perspective, it is interesting to recognize the technological awareness and competence of many youths who are economically disadvantaged. Often their only exposure to computers and other forms of technology come from playing arcade and video games.

The Rivera study concluded that the problem of inequality in digital media literacy must be addressed in the workplace, in schools, and at home. Businesses can lead the way in training employees to become fully functional with regard to computers and information sharing. However, a critical shortage of computers, and thus access to the Internet, still exists in schools and low-income homes and remains a social problem to be solved.

Public officials are working with business and education leaders to increase access to information and communications technologies in grades K–12. The notion that children need to become digitally literate if they expect to navigate in the Information Age is widely accepted. But, once again, technology is marching faster than efforts to keep up. Many employers provide digital skills training to bring current employees up to speed with information and communication technology. In the future, they will expect new hires to arrive digitally literate. Those with the greatest exposure to computers and online communications, both inside and outside of school, will have a distinct advantage in the job market. Conversely those from communities where access is limited, will become increasingly disadvantaged by comparison.

New companies, such as K–12, Inc., financed by Michael Milken and spearheaded by former Secretary of Education, William Bennett and operated by President Ron Packard, are addressing new dimensions in e-learning through their company. K–12 has a focus on home schooling.

The National Telecommunications Information Administration of the Department of Commerce issued a report titled "Falling Through the Net: *A Report on Telecommunications and the Information Technology Gap in America.*" There is nothing inherently surprising in the report. However, the report throws another wrench into the gears of equalizing media literacy. As if low income weren't enough of an obstacle, those for whom English is not the primary language face an even greater challenge in becoming competitively literate in the world of digital information and communications technology.

Schools, libraries, community groups, and businesses are responding to the challenge and trying to close the gap. Companies that can muster a solution to this dilemma through Web-based learning and other distance education devices will help grow their potential employee pool, better educate the employees they have now, and have an outstanding chance of retaining the best workers. Part of the message is that information technology is a tool and a mechanism—not an end in itself. The more individuals are taught to use the tool to access subjects of interest and benefit to themselves, the more they will use the resources that educators, librarians, community groups, and businesses are trying to make available. Claremont Graduate University is one example of a university with a strong teacher education program addressing these issues. The Fielding Graduate Institute is a distance learning university whose program is quite tutorial, but the program operates in a very distributed manner. The Fielding Model is high touch, low tech, fully accredited, and a significant success in distance education.

An inescapable conclusion drawn from these and other studies is that digital literacy skills are proportionately related to "basic literacy" skills. Those who lack essential academic literacy correspondingly lack digital literacy. Not surprisingly, those with the greatest mastery of reading, writing, and mathematics tend to also possess the highest mastery of digital information and communications skills. As we have known for some time, the greater a parent's interest and participation is a child's education, the better the child will perform academically. Joseph Loeb, CEO of BreakAway Technologies, specializing in teaching computers to low-income students, asserts, "Children who see their parents reading have a higher interest in reading themselves. This same principle applies to digital literacy. The more a child sees his or her parent(s) using computers and online resources, at work and/or at home, the greater the likelihood that the child will demonstrate proficiency in the same activities."

Closing the gap between what the River Institute report calls the "info rich" and the "info poor" is one of the greatest social challenges since the early days of the civil rights movement in America. Digital media and communications technology have a significant contribution to make with respect to literacy in its many forms.

Unplugging the Computer

It was not so very long ago that the term "wired generation" was considered futuristic. The fact that GE (General Electric) technology continuously monitors thousands of its installed medical devices serving patients around the world via the Web was also big news a few years ago. Today, being "wired" evokes thoughts of being tied down for some. Cell phones allow mobility without losing contact with the rest of the world. Other emerging technologies are making all the benefits of computing available with no wires attached. You can track a FedEx package, conclude a multinational trade agreement, pay for your newspaper subscription, and take and send photos from your palm computer.

The increasing life of batteries and the increasing quality

of heads-up displays and microphones make it possible for hands-on people, like mechanics and inspectors, to use computerized resources and conduct wireless conversations without breaking away from their work. Advancing technology that allows nearly unlimited access to digital resources opens up new opportunities for previously un-thought-of applications. With the possibilities limitless, we must think less about a wired world and more in terms of a *connected* world in health, government, education, and commerce.

Summary

This chapter has made the case that the Internet, new media, and World Wide Web are central to the future of education and workforce training. These advances should be considered in the context of other powerful trends including advances in bio-technology, globalization, the multinational nature of companies in the shrinking world, the speed of change, English as the universal language of commerce, global economies, and the changing definitions of literacy. Clearly, the Internet changes everything. Everything changes everything and global convergence and the 'Net are fundamental in shaping global learning.

The Emerging
Corporate University

Walt Disney was an early corporate leader who embraced the idea of formal and informal learning as a means of intentionally spreading enterprise-wide organizational culture. Disney spent decades cultivating and refining the corporate culture he envisioned, and then set about protecting it. Long-time Disney employees still say, "There's a right way, a wrong way, and the Disney way." When Mike Vance, Creative Thinking Association of America founder, joined the staff at Disney Studios in Burbank, California, Walt assigned a studio veteran to mentor him for a full year to ensure that Mike adopted the Disney way.

In the late 1950s and early 1960s the corporate culture at Walt Disney Productions typified its founder's management style and core beliefs. When teenage British actress Hailey Mills came to Burbank to act in her first Disney film, Walt gave her a personal tour of the studio. He showed his young star where the writers worked, let her watch the cell painters, in the animation department, and let her look over the shoulders of the carpenters and the model makers. After visiting the wardrobe department, the scenic designers, and a dozen other areas, Hailey turned to look up at Walt and asked, "What do *you* do here, Mr. Disney?"

Mike Vance, had accompanied Hailey and Walt on their tour and he explained to the young actress that Walt Disney was like a bumblebee. He described how the studio head went from department to department to monitor progress, lend creative input, and assistance to the many artists and specialists working on the family-oriented productions. Walt supported and encouraged his people do what they did best and it was his job to bring all of their creativity and talent together behind his vision and the Disney name.

Vance became the first dean of the Disney University. What had been essentially a one-to-one mentoring program became formalized as plans were being drawn up for Walt Disney World in Orlando, Florida. Walt Disney lamented that the enormous workforce the new theme park required did not know or understand the Disney culture that he had so carefully cultivated it over the years. Mike Vance kicked the development of Disney University into high gear and created workforce training courses called "Disney Way I" and "Disney Way II," for use depending on the employment level.

Corporate culture reflecting the Disney way of doing things was considered so important to the organization that all Florida employees attended Disney Way classes for a minimum of two days before they worked in *any* aspect of Walt Disney World. Operators of earth-moving equipment who worked for subcontractors of subcontractors sat through two days of Disney enlightenment before they moved so much as a shovel-full of dirt. Everyone was included…and it worked. Walt Disney died at Saint Joseph's Hospital located across the street from his Burbank studios in 1966, more than five years before the Florida property opened for business. However, Disney culture was so deeply rooted that employees say Walt still ran that company for decades after his passing. Unquestionably, Disney University was the cornerstone perpetuating the accumulated knowledge and unique style that became the hallmark of family entertainment throughout the world. Through the years, I have spoken with Frank Wells, Bill Mechanic, Brad Auerbach, and Brad Marks, all former

Disney executives who are disciples of the Disney learning culture and who have moved to significant positions in the entertainment industry. In addition, my colleague Dr. Jean Pierre Isbouts produced the seminal documentary on Walt Disney and my brother, Richard, was an attorney for Frank Wells before his passing, so I have had a great deal of contact with this evolution.

Corporate Universities in Transition

Jeanne Meister, President of Corporate University Exchange, has been a consistent advocate of the corporate university movement for many years. Corporate universities began to visibly emerge in 1955 with the launch of General Electric's Crotonville learning program. The workforce training and education landscape has changed considerably. Corporate learning centers of the past were actual campuses or places set aside for learning. Even though some corporate universities are housed in state-of-the-art facilities, the concept of the corporate university is becoming known more as a process than a physical place and e-learning is becoming a significant dimension in the programs offered.

Digital communications and the Internet are facilitating the transformation of learning from a fixed time and place event to an anytime, anywhere opportunity. Driven by the growing need for skilled, knowledgeable employees and increasing globalization, corporate classrooms are becoming virtual learning infrastructures that enable organizations to "leverage new opportunities, enter new global markets, develop deeper customer relationships, and propel the organization to a new future."

In 1988 there were approximately 400 corporate universities. Today there are more than 2,000 in the United States alone, and the number is growing. If the trend continues, the number of corporate universities could eventually exceed the number of traditional universities in the United States by 2010. The number of corporate universities in Europe is also growing. In addition to training employees, corporate universities are also becoming profit centers responsible for training a corporation's complete ecosystem or supply chain—including customers, partners, channel partners, and suppliers. Serving the value chain ensures proper representation of the corporation's products and services, and captures future e-commerce revenues. The reach of many corporate universities is global in that all of the Fortune 500 companies have international infrastructures. These companies are casting the web over global learning.

Corporate University Explosion

Disney University, General Electric's Croton-on-the-Hudson, McDonald's Hamburger U, and other corporate universities at AT&T, Hewlett-Packard, McKinsey & Company are only the tip of the iceberg. According to Corporate University Xchange, the number of corporate universities has quadrupled in less than fourteen years. The powerful, profit-driven movement toward expanding and enhancing knowledge in the workplace is just gearing up. The concept of the corporate university is now emerging in a way that has captured the interest of the international corporate culture.

Fifty percent of Fortune 500 companies now have their own universities. The general feeling among CEOs is that the number will increase each year until it will be hard to find a major organization *without* a corporate university of the same type. The benefits are significant, even though it is still difficult to get a definitive or comprehensive fix on the financial rewards in many cases and the nature of their present incarnations is quite diverse.

There are now many observable changes in human behavior as a result of corporate learning. Leaders recognize that changing people's behavior in the manner that best suits the organization's goals and objectives is important. As author and self proclaimed "accelerationist" Danny Cox, says, in his lectures, "The bottom line gets better once all of the other lines get better." An accelerationist is simply one who follows his Gestalt, is confident in moving forward, knowing that every small advance moves one toward an objective which, in the context of economic benefit, is known as "the bottom line." Many CEO's with whom I have spoken are convinced that their training investment falls to the "bottom line."

Celebrities Step Up

Despite all of the lofty language associated with the monumental changes taking place on the learning landscape, we should not forget those who talked about for-profit learning in the first place. Zig Ziglar, Dennis Waitley, Wayne Dyer, Tommy Hopkins and Michael Goldsmith, Tom Peters, and I have been selling knowledge for decades. Motivational speakers, as they are known, got the ball rolling by offering real-life learning with immediate and tangible business applications. Motivational speakers may increase sales and productivity, but the academic establishment has not paid much attention to them.

Given general academy attitude toward the fast-paced, often flamboyant style of sales trainers and motivators, a number of the first learning celebrities to enter the corporate e-learning arena are not associated with the academic world. There are, however, a number of respected academics who have now made quite an impact. Management guru Peter Drucker, a Professor at Claremont Graduate University for many years and a widely published popular author, is now online thanks to Alexander Brigham and his Phoenix-based Corpedia, Inc. Corpedia offers thirty hours of online courses based on Drucker's philosophy of organizational management. At the time they struck their arrangement, Drucker was ninety years old and Brigham only thirty-one, which is an illustration of how experience can meet innovation in the virtual world.

Corpedia, founded in 1998, first produced legal compliance programs on subjects such as sexual harassment and the Foreign Corrupt Practices Act. These programs are still marketed to corporate legal departments that want to educate employees about companies' liabilities. Brigham, who has a background in investment banking, targeted corporate learning because he recognized that corporate visionaries, no matter how talented, face a difficult challenge in disseminating expertise and instilling company pride across large, and often dispersed, workforces. Brigham sees the Internet as a valuable tool to deliver what the top corporate movers and shakers want their people to know.

The interactive online management courses from Corpedia feature Drucker's voice. Learners are presented with multiple-choice questions. If the learner clicks on the right answer, Drucker says "excellent" or "very good" in his Viennese accent. If the learner chooses incorrectly, the good professor intones, "sorry, you are wrong." Learners set goals for themselves and online instructors hold students' feet to the fire via e-mail. Corpedia, Inc. offers a certificate for successful course completion. The company hopes to upgrade that to an accredited M.B.A. Enroute to accomplishing that, Brigham is signing other well-respected names who also span both the corporate world and academia, like University of Southern California's distinguished professor, Warren Bennis. In addition, some academics such as C. Edward Demming, who stimulated quality circles and Marshall MacLuhan, known for his visions regarding media, have become Icons. I have had the good fortune to work with each of these great leaders over the years.

It seems everyone, from Steven Covey's organization in Utah to Phillip Crosby's Quality College in Florida, is now expanding their online presence. Soon, there will be expertise from every well-known specialist available, in some form or another, online. Without disrespect to our colleagues in academia, many of the most exciting new developments in learning are happening in the world of business. Perhaps that is why so many new partnerships are springing up between academic institutions and private sector corporations. Corporate universities are coming of age, thanks in part to advances in information technology and the increased knowledge those advances demand. Best practices in corporate learning are fast becoming the competitive advantages top executives strive for.

Interactive distance learning (IDL) technology, with its audio, video, graphics, and interactive capacity, is getting more exciting all the time. The ability of corporate leaders to deliver consistent and reinforceable messages is becoming easier as new online courses and programs roll out faster and less expensively than ever before. Best practices themselves can be shared online more easily and more effectively, between more people, than they could in the past. The instructional design and content issues that we discuss in this book are all formed by the plethora of new techniques and technologies in the corporate learning arena.

Smudging the Line: New Partnerships and Ventures

The sharp lines between traditional education and corporate learning are beginning to blur as education companies sell to both markets. Public dollars and private dollars are all spendable dollars. This trend of selling knowledge is described very well in the following statement from the Commission on Technology and Adult Learning:

> *"The 'new economy'—whether described as the information economy, digital economy, or knowledge economy—is characterized by structural changes that have profound implications for the public policies that frame lifelong learning. These changes include industrial and occupational change, globalization, the changing nature of competition, and the progress of the information technology revolution. They place a premium on knowledge, skills, and training. In order to develop the new systems for adult education and training that will support the skills needed in the twenty-first century, we must understand the implications for radical change in the nation's traditional context for learning, that are being driven by information technology.*
>
> *"Information technology is changing access to knowledge, the process of learning, and the delivery of education and training. Teaching and learning can now take place outside of the traditional institutional and workplace-based venues for education and training that are anchored in accreditation and certification and tied to defined skills, jobs, and career paths. Within this new context, the adult who has been an occasional 'student' becomes a continuous 'consumer' of knowledge*

available worldwide, anytime, and anywhere. As Employees gain control over their own learning and career development, employers face difficult challenges in training and retraining a workforce with consistent levels of skills.

"The relentless demand for new skills created by the use of information technology in work has reinforced the demand for effective and measurable—in terms of improvement and return-on-investment—education and training. In response, a dynamic market of for-profit providers is developing parallel to the existing public education and private sector training systems."

Accreditation

For all the good reasons corporate universities have been funded and operated in the past, there are more reasons emerging. Recently, corporate learning institutions such as McDonalds's Hamburger University, Volvo University, and Disney University have developed partnerships with traditional universities to offer employees accredited courses. A 1999 survey of corporate universities found that more than 50 percent were planning to use existing or future partnerships with accredited universities to enable corporations to make degree programs available to their employees in the fields of business/management, engineering/technical, computer science, and finance/accounting. Almost two thirds of the corporate universities surveyed reported already having some sort of alliance with an undergraduate university. Graduate universities like The Fielding Graduate Institute are actively developing partnerships and custom programs with corporate universities.

Internationally, Daimler Chrysler has established partnerships with various universities around the world including Harvard University in the United States, IMD in Lausanne, Switzerland, and others in Paris and Hong Kong.

Learning and Earning

Commerce and business have a vested interest in improving the quality of general education. Increased access to information on the Internet is becoming a larger factor in business success and Internet and Web issues are ever-expanding priorities in the private sector. What we did not know a decade ago is that education would become such a big business in and of itself. Established universities have now realized that they can use online courses to expand their enrollments (and tuition revenues) without expanding their physical plants.

Faculty members can also expand their earning capability without taking on more classroom obligations. They can teach online, at their own pace in self-paced online courses where a student's work, and faculty responses, are not delivered in real time. For the first time, thanks to the Internet, it is possible for many students from other countries to be educated at universities in the United States. This international marketing of education has also attracted tuition that American universities wouldn't have received in the past. We should not forget that on a humanitarian level, a great advancement for developing nations is to better educate their people, and the Internet is playing a key role in those efforts. Some alterations to the rules regarding resident foreign students have recently been proposed, but distance education techniques offer some help and exporting American education is also good for America.

The business and financial worlds are well aware of these developments and capital investment in private education and training firms has never been higher, especially among those who do business primarily over the Web. Chief Executive Officer of Cisco Systems, John Chambers, predicts that, *"E-learning is the next trend after e-commerce. It's the next killer application on the Internet."*

As noted earlier, courses are not the only opportunities available on line. There are a variety of certificates and credentials including A.A. degrees, B.A. degrees, B.S. degrees, M.B.A.s, and Ph.D.s now available online from institutions as notable as Duke University and Coastline Community College. The number of public and private institutions providing courses and degree programs are rapidly increasing. AOL, Monster Learning, and Kentucky and Virginia Virtual Universities are examples of aggregators now making information on all programs available. Aggregators are those organizations collecting and disbursing information about program audiences.

Technology Confusion @ Corporate U

Many people involved with creating and operating corporate universities are confused by the technology options that seem to be multiplying by the day. Confusion is likely to get worse before it gets better, due to a number of factors, including too much focus and passion for the technology and not enough for the learning outcome. But there are also signs that that condition is changing as will be discussed more fully in chapter 4 "Hail to the Chiefs."

Limited Experience Selecting Software

Human resource learning professionals, unlike IT professionals, generally have limited experience with the rigorous selection process helpful in choosing the most appropriate big software packages to address workforce needs. Trainers are trained to deal with people, not software.

Hardware & Software Upgrades

Solutions architects and scientists are not finished inventing the computer. "Boxes" that were state-of-the-art a few years ago are insufficient to handle many new applications in a fast and efficient manner, if they can handle them at all. People have come to expect speed and performance from their microprocessors, much as they expect speed and performance in a sports car. Keeping your organization wired to the latest hardware technology can be complicated and expensive. It is important to identify the role that digital technology plays in your organization before trying to hack through the sometimes mysterious and frightening hardware jungle. Even with the emergence of chief knowledge officers and the like, we don't see the importance of IT executives diminishing anytime soon. The integrated solution, the set-top box, the "lean forward," "lean back," and built-in wireless players are now here and getting better every day.

Advances in software capabilities outpace advances in hardware capabilities. Upgrades are confusing. Moreover, upgrading software is almost universally faster and less expensive than changing outdated hardware. As software evolves, it can store, retrieve, and process data at an ever-increasing speed. That's why IT professionals play a critical role in matching an organization's software needs to the realities of its hardware limitations.

Making the Transition

Lakewood Research of Minneapolis, Minnesota, conducted an End-of-Millennium Training Industry Survey, which provided a snapshot of corporate learning at the millennium and contains some helpful information for those trying to determine how to position learning issues on their corporation's priority list. One item of note is the increasing compensation for internal learning staffs. With the intense scrutiny that budgets receive in both for-profit and non-profit organizations, it is safe to conclude that more and more executive decision-makers are coming to appreciate the vital roles knowledge and information are playing in their success. As further testament to this important trend, the study showed that the amount of funding appropriated for the purchase of outside goods and services for learning is also increasing significantly.

Classrooms with live instructors are still the learning mainstay in 90 percent of the organizations surveyed. But the amount and variety of technology-based media is growing rapidly. Workbooks and manuals are used in 74 percent of the surveyed companies, and 69 percent use videotapes. None of these figures is surprising because corporate learning departments are built in the image of corporate trainers. Public seminars, role-playing, non-computerized games, and other traditional learning practices are still frequently used.

Classroom instruction, manuals, and videotapes have been found in abundance in corporate classrooms, just as in public classrooms, for the past quarter century. That is the environment and the tools corporate educators know best. The End-of-Millennium Training Industry Survey, however, included some items that weren't even on the map for much of the past twenty-five years. Computer-based learning media, such as CD-ROMs, etc., were being used in 54-four percent of the responding organizations. Internet-delivered learning was being used in 36 percent of the organizations. If this were Billboard Magazine there would be a bullet beside the latter.

Compared to corporate learning as a whole, Internet-delivered learning is still in its infancy. Level one technical learning, the use of non-Internet computer learning resources, was evident in more than half of the surveyed organizations. Learning on level two is defined as the emerging use of Internet learning resources. The availability of Internet learning programs and materials is on the rise and the ability to negotiate the Web reflects a more intimate merger between user and technology. The mere appearance of Internet-delivered learning represents an acknowledged major trend.

In a self-fulfilling prophecy, the Internet itself is fueling the increasing hunger for the Web's vast stores of knowledge. Never before has learning taken on such proportions, due in part to availability, speed, and ease of access, and a growing sense of authority. Advertisers once used the slogan "As seen on TV" to infer credibility. Now, if it's found on the Web, there is an implicit validity and reliability to the information for some people. Another major factor distinguishing the Internet is its power to research, cross-reference, and verify information. Television never offered that.

IBM Corporation released a television commercial in 2000 that said, "How many Libraries of Congress can your software handle per second?" It is difficult to conceive of the amount of information that exists in cyberspace, and difficult to understand how little of it we have accessed.

The Problem and the Solution Rolled Into One

Some corporate infrastructure for performance improvement has become necessary. Many of the challenges facing business today did not exist a decade ago. New technology is at the core of these changes. Advances in digital communications have shrunk the globe. It is now necessary to inform, educate, and communicate with geographically diverse organizational populations. The best way to do that is to use e-learning models that link communities of interest, professional practice, and culture.

Studies have revealed that the use of e-learning has diminished travel expenses historically associated with off-campus learning. Similar cost benefits are appearing on the corporate campus, as well. These are opportunity costs for employers. In many cases e-learning is proving to be faster, just-in-time, and used more often on the learner's time than conventional modes of corporate learning. Continuous development and improvement of hardware and courseware is taking place and content updates are becoming faster, easier, and less expensive as well. General Electric and other corporations have switched almost entirely to e-learning. An impressive 20 percent of all corporate learning took place electronically in 1999 and it is predicted that more than 40 percent of corporate learning will be electronic by the end of 2010.

Much of the electronic learning activity referred to consists of CD-ROMs, DVD and videotapes but the Internet is quickly establishing itself as a major access mechanism for electronic learning. DVD and I-DVD are opening the way to new strategies. In 1999, 92 percent of major corporations surveyed were testing Web-based learning with an eye to substantially reduce learning costs, most specifically, travel expenses. This e-learning strategy, including the Internet and new media, is the burgeoning new dimension of corporate learning.

The unique and valuable benefit of interactivity, the ability to monitor learners' progress, or lack of progress, is immensely helpful to instructors and enables them to respond to learners' needs faster and more effectively. The e-learner's grasp of a subject and level of retention can be easily tracked.

Content and Access: The One-Two Punch

Marshall McLuhan determined that the medium is

primarily the message. Digital communication technology is not the message. The message is the message. Philips and Sony Corporations are in the final stages of developing a compact disc with ten to twenty times the storage capacity of today's DVDs. The message is in the *content.*

It is common for new developments in technology to grab headlines. As the media continues to evolve, so must the content. With new broadband and wireless technologies, new and exciting e-learning experiences are imminent. More and more online learning providers are offering customized programs to clients. E-learning enterprises create and host tailored programs for specific companies. Technology is basically neutral; the richness is found in the content.

VCampus, an online learning provider, is using the ASP model to offer a virtual campus to corporations and universities. The company or school can then provide workers or students with access to the virtual campus, which includes tools for recording student scores, rating courses, and *developing content.* VCampus and similar organizations are meeting the business-to-business, or B2B, online learning demand with solutions that are faster and less expensive than what a company or college would pay to develop the technology and content.

Learning is the Key

Using General Electric as a model, we can examine what a true learning organization looks like, how it thinks, and how it acts. An organization is a community of living humans. That means that what helps people to grow and develop also helps the organization to improve. Learning leads to success and underscores the Global Learning Systems motto: "Earning through learning."

General Electric is both large and diverse. It has 250 business divisions, thirteen of which are Fortune 500 size. The better organizations become at sharing information via digital technology, the faster individual employees, and in turn the organizations, improve. GE Medical Systems developed remote diagnostics capabilities, which are applications of digital communications technology. Using remote diagnostics, installed equipment can be monitored from the manufacturer's site. They can detect and even repair an impending malfunction before the customer even knows there is a problem.

This remote diagnostic technology is shared among all GE business units and, as a result, jet aircraft engines are monitored in flight, railroad locomotives are monitored as they haul freight, power plant turbines, equipment in paper mills, and other industrial motors and systems are likewise monitored for performance and preventive maintenance. All of these functions are digital communications applications.

Often organizations learn from the outside in, meaning that they learn how they can improve, as well as how much they need to improve, from the world in which they operate. General Electric's former CEO, Jack Welch, described the successful executive as one who accepts that there is more than one way to do something, even if s/he hasn't discovered the best alternatives yet. The thirst for knowledge requires learning that reaches outside of any single organization.

There is Help Out There

One key to the success of any corporate university is access. A corporate university is much more than an enhanced training department. One of its purposes is to enable corporations to brand the learning initiatives into which they invest significant capitol. If the corporation chooses to, the educational programs, courseware, and processes can usually be packaged for other firms to use. More and more companies are realizing, as Walt Disney did many years ago, that a university is a powerful force in creating and sustaining corporate culture. Author and leadership expert Margaret Wheatley likes to say, "culture happens," no matter what you do. So you might as well be intentional about it.

Corporate University Xchange, Inc. identified the following reasons for organizations to launch universities:

• A desire to link learning and development to business goals

• The creation of a systematic approach for learning and development

- To spread common values across the organization
- Develop the human capital that the organization has at its disposal
- To increase their competitive position in the market

All of the reasons to establish and sustain a corporate university can be enhanced through digital technology. Given the many benefits and advantages that we've discussed to this point, all of the desirable outcomes mentioned may be assisted and improved by online electronic communications. Even in organizations that consider themselves as far from e-commerce as they can be, there is virtually no aspect of corporate life that is not powerfully affected by Internet and intranet activities.

What Drives Corporate Universities?

In the knowledge economy, corporate universities and learning organizations are playing mission-critical roles within the corporation. Cost containment, downsizing, and strategic change are factors that affect who we train and how we train. While some learning organizations still take traditional classroom approaches, others are using the benefits of e-learning to meet corporate objectives. E-learning implementations within companies include using technology to train individuals to use technology, new product introductions, tracking regulatory compliance, on-demand task or skill references, degree programs from online universities, and IT certifications.

If knowledge is a corporate asset, then learning must be viewed as both a strategic initiative and competitive advantage. One sign that learning has come of age is the advent of the corporate university and the CLO, i.e., Chief Learning Officer. In many cases the CLO, reporting to the chief executive officer, is a lateral position to the chief financial officer and the CLO participates when the executive team plans future strategy. The role of various corporate officers will be discussed in greater detail in chapter 4.

Globalization of the Workforce

Globalization of the workforce is more than an abstract and entertaining concept. The future is here. Multi-national airline partnerships, like American's One World program, are a direct reflection of how national boundaries are being smudged or sometimes erased altogether by corporate mergers, acquisitions, and alliances. Dealing with these new geographical and cultural challenges is serious business. Professor Thomas L. Friedman states:

> *"Globalization isn't a choice. It's a reality. There is just one global market today, and the only way you can grow at the speed [you] want to grow is to tap into the global stock and bond markets, by seeking out multinationals to invest in your company, and by selling into the global trading system."*

The complete flexibility of e-learning also spans time zones. Not only are local languages an issue for course designers, so are local customs. The flexibility of e-learning can accommodate those types of specifics. We recommend that you think globally as you read and digest the information and ideas in this book. Let your context of understanding go beyond traditional borders.

Time-to-Market

Time-to-market is also a major driver for corporations. When your company is global and product-launch information needs to reach thousands of sales, support, and management professionals who are decentralized (perhaps around of the world), instructor-led learning might not be able to provide the speed necessary to maximize return on investment. The product may be available for sale, but if salespeople are not informed, opportunities are lost and the door is opened for a faster, better informed competitor to react.

The Bottom Line

According to *Training Magazine*, corporations save between 50 and 70 percent when they replace instructor-led learning with alternative electronic delivery. Housing and travel costs account for the majority of the savings. Lost productivity and lost revenue can actually be higher if you consider that classroom days include not only travel time, but also total time away from the office. And what is the cost of looking for information? Savings from *just-in-time* reference tools may be difficult to accurately assess, but should be considered in the cost-savings calculations.

Modular e-learning is another source of cost savings that allows learning to be spread out over a period of several days. This flexibility allows the student to attend to business and then learn when he/she has the time to concentrate. The company benefits as the employee keeps work on schedule, and the student benefits by progressing with valuable course work.

Timing is Everything

Compare strategic learning to *just-in-case* training that is not necessarily tied to specific corporate objectives. Training in this category simply becomes an event with little immediate relevance to the employee. While some information will be retained immediately following the course, over longer periods of time, knowledge retention dissipates. The Research Institute of America found that thirty-three minutes after a lecture is completed students usually retain only 58 percent of the material covered. By the second day 33 percent is retained and three weeks after the lecture is completed only 15 percent of the knowledge is retained.

How Long Will Corporate Universities Last?

The corporate university is now a vertical segment of the education industry. I defined verticals as higher, adult, and community college segments. There is no doubt that these are revolutionary times and intelligence and knowledge will not be reverting to its previous "backseat" position in organizational life. The Internet and all that emerging digital communications technology has to offer will carry the information economy past the foreseeable horizon and it well become the communications economy. Those organizations that offer integrated solutions will provide the flexibility and depth that organizations need to make prudent, sensible, and cost-effective investments in both individual and organizational knowledge. The corporate university is here to stay and will continue to grow in the future.

What Needs to Change and What Needs to Remain the Same?

There are about 3,000 accredited colleges and universities in the United States, 1,300 community colleges and 2,000 corporate universities. So, the corporate university has now risen in stature and has become a vertical segment of significance in the education industry.

The "Corporate University" is a title for whatever a company needs or wants it to be. It may be large and general, or narrow and specific. It may be part of an HR operation or quite independent. It may be headed by a CLO, a Dean, a manager, or a director. The point is, the mechanism for corporate education and training is growing and going online.

The next chapter provides a list of approximately 100 corporate universities, which will give a sense of scope and dimension to this emerging phenomenon.

Examples of Corporate Universities

This Chapter identifies many corporate universities. Although the "Corporate University" is a metaphor, some have formal class facilities, including lecture halls and learning laboratories, augmented by hotel accommodations and recreational facilities and beautiful grounds. The majority of these initiatives are now adding distributed learning opportunities, many of which are being "outsourced."

Examples of the corporate universities with campus facilities are Southwest Airlines Peoples University, General Electric and Xerox. Xerox Document University, a beautifully designed and maintained campus, was sold by Xerox and is now an independent conference and training center, which Xerox continues to use for some of its training requirements. In addition, its corporate university, Xerox Management Institute, provides leadership education and training for the company's managers.

General Electric, at its Management Development Institute in Crotonville, NY, teaches and trains its managers in GE corporate culture and leadership. Former GE President Jack Welch, before his retirement was so committed to this process that he spent one day a month on campus to teach and meet with the students.

Motorola University is the strategic learning organization of a corporation. As of this writing Motorola University has become troubled and its fate is unclear.

There are numbers of corporate universities that operate without a campus, existing only on the web. NationalCity Online Learning Center offers free financial services courses, as do WebStreetUniversity, and Bloomberg University. Powered, Inc., created each of these virtual universities, and was formerly called notHarvard.com. Each of these virtual universities was outsourced and in each case the target audience is the company's customers or potential customers. Educating the customer is becoming an important function.

This chapter provides examples of the varieties and types of corporate universities.

Corporations with Training Centers, Corporate Universities

AB University

Anheuser-Busch
1Busch Place
St. Louis, MO 63118
(317)577-3858
www.anheuser-busch.com
employees, customers
and suppliers

Academie Accor

Accor S.A.
1, rue de la Mare Neuve
91 021 Evry Cedex, France
Tel.   01 69 36 86 00
Fax. 01 60 79 45 36
www.accor.com
employees and
open hospitality training

Aetna Institute for Corporate Education

Aetna, Inc.
151 Farming Avenue S. 124
Hartford, CT 06156-1000
(860) 273-0123
www.aetna.com
employees only

Air University

United States Air Force
55 Lamay Playa South
Maxwell Air Force Base
Montgomery, AL 36112
(334) 953-1110
www.au.af.mil
professional military

Amdahl University

Amdahl Corporation
1250 East Arques Avenue
Sunnyvale, CA 94088
(408) 746-6000
www.amdahl.com

American Express Quality University

American Express
Company
20022 North 31st Avenue
Phoenix, AZ
(602)537-8500
www.americanexpress.com
employees only

American Skandia University

3 Corporate Drive
Shelton, CT 06484
(203)926-1888
www.americanskandia.com
employees only

Amoco Management Learning Center

BP Amoco Corporation
2001 Butterfield Road,
Suite 150
Downer's Grove, IL 60515
(708) 241-8021
www.bpamoco.com
employees and clients

AMS University

American Management
Systems
4000 Legato Road
Fairfax, VA 22033
(703) 267-8000
www.amsinc.com/
aboutams /amsu
employees only

Apple University

Apple Computer, Inc.
Mailstop 84-3CE
1 Infinite Loop
Cupertino, CA 95014
(408) 996-1010
www.apple.com
employees only

**Arthur Anderson
Center for Professional
Development**

Arthur Anderson & Co
1405 North Fifth Avenue
St. Charles, IL 60174-1264
(630) 444-5320
www.arthuranderson.com
employees and clients

**Arthur D. Little
School of Management**

Arthur D. Little
194 Beacon Street
Chestnut Hill, MA 02467
(617)552-2877
www.adlittle.com
one year accredited MS
(Management) program
& executive education
employees and clients

**The AT&T
Learning Center**

AT&T Corp.
300 North Maple Avenue
Basking Ridge, NJ 07920
(800) ATT-CNTR
www.attlearningcenter.com
employees only

Bank One University

Bank One Corporation
2500 Westfield Drive
Elgin, IL 60123
(800) 930-1111
www.bankone.com
employees only

**Bank of Montreal
Institute for Learning**

Bank of Montreal
3550 Pharmacy Ave.
Scarborough, Ontario
M1W-3Z3
CANADA
(416) 0490-4494
www.bmo.com
employees only

Bechtel University

Bechtel Group, Inc.
50 Beale Street
San Francisco, CA 94119
415-228-4349
www.bechtel.com
employees only

BOCA Campus On-Line

Building Officials and Code
Administrators
International, Inc.

4051 West Flossmoor Road
Country Club Hills,
IL 60478
(708) 799-2300
www.icccampus.org
open code enforcement
courses, online BS
(Administration) degree
program in co-operation
with Central Michigan
University

**Bristol-Myers Squibb
Pharmaceutical College**

Bristol-Myers Squibb
Company
100 Headquarters Park Drive
Skillman, NJ 08558
(609) 252-4000
www.bms.com

Bulab Learning Center

Buckman Laboratories
1256 North McLean Blvd.
Memphis, TN 38108
1-800-BUCKMAN
blcenter@buckman.com
at this time only
employees

Cable & Wireless College

Cable & Wireless plc
320 Westwood Heath Road
Coventry, West Midlands
CV4 8GP
United Kingdom
(44) 20 7135 4000
www.cwplc.com
employees only

**Centro Internacional de
Educación y Desarrollo**

Petróleos De Venezuela
Av. Intercomunal La
Trinidad-El Hatillo Con
Calle El Angel De La
Tahona Urb.
Las Esmeraldas,
Caracas 1083 Venezuela
www.pdv.com
employee management
education

Charles Schwab University

The Charles Schwab
Corporation
101 Montgomery Street
San Francisco, CA 94104
(800) 435-4000
www.schwab.com
employees only

**Chase Development
Center**

The Chase Manhattan
Corporation
One Chase Manhattan
Plaza
28th floor
New York, NY 10081
(212) 552-5000
www.chase.com

**Chevron Technical
University**

Chevron Corporation
575 Market St.
San Francisco, CA 94105
(415) 346-5434
www.chevron.com
employees only

CIBC Leadership Centre

Canadian Imperial Bank
of Commerce
12750 Jane Street
RRI
King City, ON L7B1A3
Canada
(905) 833-3086
www.cibc.com

CMDS Team University

Computer Management and
Development Services
Post Office Box 1184
Harrisonburg, VA 22801
(540) 432-5200
www.cmds.com
employees and clients

CNA Insurance Companies

CNA Plaza
333 Wabash Avenue
Chicago, IL 60685
(312) 822-5000
www.cna.com
employees only

**The Coca-Cola Company
Learning Center**

The Coca-Cola Company
P.O. Box 1734
Atlanta, GA 30301
(404) 676-8900
www.coca-cola.com
employees only

**College Center of the
Finger Lakes**

Corning Incorporated
One Riverfront Plaza

Corning, NY 14831
(607) 974-9000
www.corning.com
employees and customers

CostCo University

CostCo Wholesale
Corporation
999 Lake Drive
Issaquah, WA 98027
(425) 313-8100
www.costco.com

**UAW/DaimlerChrysler
National Training Center**

DaimlerChrysler
Corporation
2211 East Jefferson Avenue
Detroit, MI 48207
(313) 567-3300
www.daimlerchrysler.com/e
employees only

**Dana Customer Training
Center**

Dana Corporation
8000 Yankee Road
Ottawa Lake, MI 49267
(419) 535-4300
www.dana.com
employees and customers

**Defense Acquisition
University**

Department of Defense
9820 Belvoir Road
Ft. Belvoir, VA 22060
(703) 805-3360
www.dau.mil
military and civilian
professionals

Dell University

Dell Computer Corporation
2214 West Braker Lane
Austin, TX 78758-4053
(512) 338-4000
www.dell.com
employees only

Disney Institute

Post Office Box 3232
Anaheim, CA 92803
(714) 781-4433
or P.O. Box 10,000
Lake Buena Vista, FL
32830-1000
disney.go.com/Disney
World/DisneyInstitute/
ProfessionalPrograms
www.disneyseminars.com
employees only

Dow Employee Development Center

The Dow Chemical
Company
2030 Willard H. Dow Ctr
Midland, MI 48674-0001
(5170 636-1000
www.dow.com
employees only

Dow Leadership Development Center

The Dow Chemical
Company
22 East Galloway Drive
Hillsdale, MI 49242
(517) 437-3311
www.dow.com
employees only

DuPont Quality Management & Technology Center

E I DuPont de Nemours
and Company
1007 Market St.
Wilmington, DE 19898
(302) 774-2414
www.dupont.com
employees only

Eaton School of Retailing

The T. Eaton Company, Ltd.
250 Young Street
Toronto, Ontario M5B 1O8
Canada
(416) 598-8700
www.eatons.com
employees and paying
students

Employee Development University

Southern California Water
Company
630 East Foothill Blvd.
San Dimas, CA 91773-1207
(909) 394-3600 ext.777
www.eduniv.com
employees and paying
students

Ericsson University, North America

Ericsson, Inc.
6300 Legacy Drive
Plano, TX 75024
(972) 583-0000
www.ericsson.com

Eddie Bauer University

Eddie Bauer, Inc.
P.O. Box 97000
Redmond, WA 98073
(425) 882-6100
www.thespiegelgroup.com

Factory Mutual Conference Center

Factory Mutual Insurance Company
1151 Boston Providence Highway
Norwood, MA 02062
(781) 769-7900
www.factorymutual.com

Federal Express Leadership Institute

Federal Express Corporation
3035 Directors Row
Memphis, TN 38131
(901) 398-1111
www.fedexcorp.com
FedEx managers only

Fidelity Investments Retail Training Services

FMR Corp.
82 Devonshire Street
Boston, MA 02109
(617) 563-7000
www.fidelity.com

First University

First Union Corporation
301 South College Street
Charlotte, NC 28288-0957
(704) 383-1971
www.firstunion.com
employees only

Flagship University

American Airlines
4501 Highway 360
Fort Worth, TX 76155
(817)963-6905
www.amrcorp.com
employees only

Ford Fairlane Training and Development Center

Ford Motor Company
1900 Hubbard Drive
Dearborn, MI 48121
www.ford.com
(888) 993-3673
employees only

Ford Heavy Truck University

Ford Motor Company
100 Renaissance Center
Detroit, MI 48243
www.ford.com
employees only

FORDSTAR

Ford Motor Company
330 Towne Center Drive
Dearborn, MI 48126
(800) 392-3673
www.ford.com
digital satellite network for dealer & technician training

GE Management Development Institute

General Electric Corporation
Old Albany Post Road
Ossining, NY 10562
(914) 944-2100

www.ge.com
employees only, required
participation by all GE
managers

General Motors University

General Motors
Corporation
100 Renaissance Center
Detroit, MI 48265
(313) 556-5000
www.gm.com
employees only (company
culture change agent)

Hamburger University

McDonald's Corporation
Ronald Lane
Oak Brook, IL 60521
(630) 623-3000
www.mcdonalds.com
employees only

Harley-Davidson University

Harley-Davidson, Inc.
3700 W. Juneau Avenue
Milwaukee, WI 53208
(414) 342-4680
www.harley-davidson.com
employees, customers and
suppliers

Hart, Schaffner & Marx University

Hartmarx Corporation
101 North Wacker Drive
Chicago, IL 60606
(312) 372-6300
www.hartmarx.com
accredited program (CEU)
for employees and clients

Hitachi Institute of Management Development

Hitachi, Ltd.
4-6 Kanda Surugadai
Chiyoda-ku
Tokyo, Japan 101-8010
(+81) 3-3258-1111
www.hitachi.co.jp

Iams University

The Iams Company
7250 Poe Avenue
Dayton, OH 45414
(800) 525-4267
www.iams.com
employees and distribution
chain

IBM Global Learning

IBM Corporation
New Orchard Road
Armonk, NY 10504
(914) 499-1900
www.ibm.com
over 10,000 employee
courses

Intel University

Intel Corporation
2565 Walsh Avenue
Santa Clara, CA 95051
(408) 765-6080
www.intel.com
employees only

Jefferson Wells Corporate University

Jefferson Wells
International, Inc.
825 North Jefferson Street,
Suite 200

Milwaukee, WI 53202
(800) 826-5099
www.jefferson-wells.com
employee & courses for
paying accountants, internal
auditors, & tax professionals

**John Hancock
Conference Center**

John Hancock Financial
Services, Inc.
40 Trinity Place
Boston, MA 02116
(617) 572-7700
www.jhancock.com
employees & general agents
only

John Deere University

Deere & Company
1175 E. 90th Street
Davenport, IA 52809
(319) 388-4501
www.deere.com
employees & preferred
customers

Johnson Controls Institute

Johnson Controls Inc.
507 E. Michigan Avenue,
M-45
Milwaukee, WI 53202
(800) 524-8540
www.johnsoncontrols.com
employees & paying
students

Land Rover University

Land Rover, North America
10100 Business Parkway
Lanham, MD 20706

(301) 731-8155
www.landrover.com
employees only

**Lord Institute for
Technical and
Management Training**

Lord Corporation
2000 West Grandview Blvd.
Erie, PA 16509
(814) 868-0924
www.lordcorp.com
employees and paying
students (accredited by PA
Department of Education)

Marine Corps University

United States Marine Corps
2076 South Street
Quantico, VA 22134
www.mcu.usmc.mil
military and selected
professionals

MasterCard University

MasterCard International
2000 Purchase Street #101
Purchase, NY 10577
(914) 249-2000
www.mastercard.com/
consumer/mcu/
free consumer financial
service courses

**Mashantucket Pequot
Academy**

PO Box 3057
Mashantucket, CT 06339
(860) 678-7488
www.pequotacademy.com
tribal and paying student

basic server & manager courses

MBNA Customer College

400 Christiana Road
Newark, DE 19713
(800) 441-7048
www.mbna.com
employees only

Merck University

Merck KgaA Darmstadt
Franfurterstrasse 250
64293 Darmstadt
Germany
06151/72-3745
www.merk.de
senior management
seminars for two weeks
each at WHU Koblenz,
University of Chicago,
London School of
Economics, & Hong Kong
University of Science &
Technology

Mitchell University

Mitchell International
9889 Willow Creek Road
San Diego, CA 92131
(858) 578-6550
www.mitchell.com
online training for windows-
based automotive repair
estimating system

Motorola University

Motorola, Inc.
1303 East Algonquin Road,
Sixth floor
Schaumburg, IL 60196-1097

(708) 576-3704
www.mot.com
employees and paying
students

**National Defense
University**

Department of Defense
Ft. McNair
300 5th Ave, SW, Bdg. 62
Washington, DC 20319-
5066
(202) 685-3922
www.ndu.edu
joint professional military
education

**National City Online
Learning Center**

National City Corporation
National City Center
1900 East Ninth Street
Cleveland, OH 44114
(216) 575-2000
www.nclearning.com
free financial courses

**National Semiconductor
University**

National Semiconductor
2900 Semiconductor Dr.
P.O. Box 58090
Santa Clara, CA 95052-8090
(408) 721-5000
www.national.com
employees only

**Nationwide Financial
University**

Nationwide Mutual
Insurance Company

One Nationwide Plaza
Columbus, OH 43215-2220
(614) 249-7111
www.nationwide.com
employees only

Oracle University

Oracle Corporation
500 Oracle Parkway
Redwood Shores, CA 94065
(650) 506-7000
www.oracle.com
employees and paying
students

PeopleSoft University

PeopleSoft, Inc.
4460 Hacienda Dr.
Pleasanton CA 94588-3031
(925) 225-3000
www.peoplesoft.com
employees and paying
students

Procter & Gamble University

Procter & Gamble
One Procter & Gamble
Plaza
Cincinnati, OH 45202
(513) 983-1100
www.pg.com
employees only

PTO University

U.S. Patent & Trademark
Office
2011 Crystal Drive, Suite 601
Arlington, VA 22202
(703) 308-5315
www.uspto.gov

employee professional
development

Quality Academy

Northern States Power
Company
414 Nicollet Mall
Minneapolis, MN 55401
(612) 330-5500
www.nspco.com
employees, supply and
demand chain

Raychem University

Raychem Corporation
300 Constitution Drive
Menlo Park, CA 94025-1164
(650) 361-3333
www.raychem.com

Ratheon Learning Institute

Raytheon Company
6620 Chase Oaks Blvd.
Plano, TX 75023
(972) 575-2000
www.raytheon.com
employees only

Rover Business Learning

Rover Group, Ltd.
P.O. Box 41, Longbridge
Birmingham B31 2TB
United Kingdom
www.rovergroup.uk

Saturn Training Center

100 Saturn Parkway
Spring Hill, TN 37174
(931) 486-7775
www.saturn.com

supply and distribution chains

SBC Center for Learning

Southwestern Bell Corporation
6301 Colwell Drive
Irving, TX 7503
www.sbc.com
employees only

Sears Conference & Training Center

3333 Beverly Road
Hoffman Estates, IL 60179
(847) 286-0150
www.sears.com
employees only

Service Delivery University

Fidelity Investments
82 Devonshire Street
Boston, MA 02109
(617) 563-7000
www.fidelity.com

Smith Barney Conference Center

388 Greenwich Street
26th floor
New York, NY 10013
(212) 816-6000
www.salomonsmithbarney.com
employees only

Southern Company College

64 Perimeter Center East
Atlanta, GA 30346

(404) 506-5000
www.southernco.com

Sprint University of Excellence

2330 Shawnee Mission Parkway
Westwood, KS 66205
(816) 501-8839
www.sprint.com
employees only

St. Paul University

The St. Paul Companies, Inc.
385 Washington Street
St. Paul, MN 55102
(651) 310-7911
www.stpaul.com
at this time internal only

Sterling University

Sterling Resources, Inc.
6 Forest Avenue
Paramus, NJ 07652
(201)843-6444
www.sterlinguniversity.com
employees and paying students

Sun U

Sun Microsystems
2550 Garcia Avenue
Mountain View, CA 94043
(650) 960-1300
www.sunco.com
employees only

Target Stores University

Target Corporation
33 South 6th Street
Minneapolis, MN 55402
(612) 370-6948
www.targetcorp.com
employees only

Texas Instruments Learning Institute

P.O. Box 650311, MS 3928
Dallas, TX 75265
(214) 917-1920
www.ti.com
employees only

Thomas & Betts University

Thomas & Betts
8155 T & B Boulevard
Memphis, TN 38125
(901) 252-8000
http://tbu.tnb.com/tbu
employees only

3Com University

3Com
5400 Bayfront Plaza
Santa Clara, CA 95052
(408)326-5000
www.3com.com/training/3comu
employees and paying students

TVA University

Tennessee Valley Authority
400 West Summit Hill Drive
Knoxville, TN 37902
(865) 632-2101
www.tva,gov/tvau/
employee development & professional training

UCH Academy

University of Chicago Hospitals
5841 S. Maryland Ave.
Chicago, IL 60637
(773) 753-0850
www.uchospitals.edu/academy
employees and paying students

Unisys University

Unisys Corporation
Unisys Way
Blue Bell. PA 19424
(215) 986-4011
www.unisys.com
employees only

United HealthCare Learning Institute

United HealthCare
450 Columbus Blvd.
Hartford, CT 06115
(800) 549-3166
www.unitedhealthgroup.com
internal only

University for People

Southwest Airlines
PO Box 36611
Dallas, TX 75235
(214) 792-7847
www.southwest.com
employees only

Verizon University

Verizon Communications, Inc.
1095 Avenue of the Americas
New York, NY 10036
(212) 395-2121
www.verizon.com
employees & selected customers only

Walton Institute

Wal-Mart stores
702 Southwest 8th Street
Bentonville, AR 72716-8074
(501) 273-6206
www.walmartstores.com
employees only

Whirlpool Brandywine Performance Centre

78300 County Road 378
Covert, MI 49043
(616) 923-5000
www.whirlpool.com
employee , suppliers & dealers

Workforce Development

Verizon Communications, Inc.
750 Canyon Drive
Coppell, TX 75019
(214) 285-1219
www.verizon.com
employees only

Wireless University

Lucent Technologies, Inc.
600 Mountain Avenue
Murray Hill, NJ 07974
(908) 582-8500
www.lucent.com
employee web-based training

Xerox Document University

Xerox Corporation
Post Office Box 2000
Leesburg, VA 20176
(703) 729-8000
www.xerox.com
employees and paying students

The corporate university is a metaphor and is amorphous. It can take any shape and be any size. One of its main purposes is to be a vehicle for education and training for a company. It is also an organizing vehicle for workforce training and a leadership center where the learning imperative can be nurtured to give a company its competitive edge. In my view it is a good and workable structure. Corporate universities will continue to grow in number and the variety of types will increase.

My special thanks to Peter Goldschmidt for his efforts in helping tremendously in gathering the information in this Chapter.

Hail to the Chiefs

Leadership is the key to workforce training

If you have only recently heard the term "Chief Knowledge Officer" you are not alone. At the time Bill Clinton was elected to his first term in the White House, there were few chief knowledge officers and little interest in the position. Their numbers were statistically insignificant. Now, over 25 percent of Fortune 500 companies have CKOs, and the percentage is growing. The emergence of the CKO, or comparable title, is a good indicator that organizational leaders are recognizing the links between knowledge, productivity, and profitability. In addition, new titles are emerging, such as Chief Learning Officer. This chapter will examine the emerging new "Chiefs."

Although estimates vary widely, there is no question that the lack of knowledge and fundamental skills in the workplace costs American and foreign businesses billions in lost productivity and opportunity each year. The literature affirms that interest and enthusiasm behind corporate education and corporate learning is increasing, yet, at present, the bleak K–12 public education pictures raises concerns over future skills and mastery limitations in the work force. The number one priority articulated by President George W. Bush in his quest for the presidency was the tremendous need to improve education. Strategies that promise to remedy the financial drain and limitations of an undereducated workforce are very popular in executive suites and at annual shareholders' meetings.

The need to develop practices and methodologies to close the skills gap is only part of the knowledge and learning equation in organizational life. Even with Edgate, K12, Inc., Edison, and other initiatives well under way to improve K–12 and secondary education, organizational leaders must deal with their present and newly hired employees "where they are" (at the knowledge and skill levels they currently possess). The need for workforce education and training looms large.

Intellectual capital is now actually beginning to achieve parity with financial capital in the pursuit of a sustainable market advantage and earnings. Organizational leaders must address the fact that intellectual assets are difficult to quantify in a world conditioned to deal strictly with financial data. Recognizing that knowledge is a prime commodity in the Age of Information, more and more companies have figured out that they must put somebody in charge of the intellectual capital of an organization. Many executives also recognize the need to cultivate a corporate climate that acknowledges knowledge for its inherent value.

Alphabet Soup

If an activity or issue is sufficiently important to the success of the organization, then its champion needs to be an individual with substantial organizational power. The trunk of the tree is the "Chief Knowledge Officer" (CKO), from which the various branches comprising the family of chiefs related to training, education, and information continue to grow and evolve.

Without leadership, education and training initiatives are regressive. Because knowledge is an increasingly vital issue, the chiefs may also be looked upon as a team of champions dedicated to the success of the corporate collective. To expand beyond the CKO, we are going to look at a variety of chiefs because each variation may have unique impact on corporate learning. Listed below are the typical responsibilities of "the chiefs"—corporate officers. All chiefs are solutions architects. The evolution is toward the inclusion and development of the CLO, Chief Learning Officer, either inside of Human Resources or as an independent function.

CEO (Chief Executive Officer)

DESCRIPTION: Perhaps the original chief designation, CEO could also stand for "chief *everything* officer." The CEO is expected to provide the ultimate leadership in an organization. Typically, the CEO's paycheck reflects "top dog" status. Because effective leadership is such a critical factor in organizational success, good CEO's deserve every penny of their often mind-boggling compensation packages. The CEO is ultimately responsible for every element in organizational life. His or her job description is truly without boundaries.

PRIMARY RESPONSIBILITIES:

- Be the public spokesperson for the organization
- Preach the gospel of the industry in which s/he is engaged
- Represent the organization to customers, analysts, and all stakeholders
- Establish a vision and direction for the organization
- Communicate the vision and direction to everyone
- Build and sustain teams that will achieve the stated goals of the organization
- Accept responsibility for organizational breakdowns and act swiftly to find and implement remedies

ROLE IN LEARNING: No single individual has more influence over the beliefs and behaviors of an organization than the CEO. Therefore the chief executive must engender a culture of learning and see to it that learning becomes part of daily life for everyone. The CEO must ensure that learning initiatives receive all necessary resources to operate properly and that the initiatives are backed by the power of his or her office. Without the full support of the CEO, organizational learning is vulnerable at best and non-existent at worst.

BACKGROUND: CEOs can come from virtually any professional background. Many tend to come out of finance, engineering, and marketing. Common CEO attributes include being aggressive, outspoken, passionate, visionary, tireless, charismatic, and innovative. In today's world interpersonal skills are becoming more and more important.

CFO (Chief Financial Officer)

DESCRIPTION: Numbers are the language of corporate life. Even with recent inclusion of qualitative considerations in valuing a company's performance, numbers still rule. We don't see that changing any time soon, especially with the Enron and Global Crossing traumas so fresh in our minds. So the CFO will remain near the top of the corporate ladder. The new development for CFOs is the way that organizational learning positively impacts corporate earnings.

PRIMARY RESPONSIBILITIES:

- Supervise all corporate financial accounting activities
- Report on the organization's financial health & performance
- Monitor expenses and the overall cost of doing business
- Advise department heads on best financial practices
- Prepare financial statements
- Spot financial trends that will effect profitability
- Predict future performance
- Ensure that the organization's financials are properly audited

ROLE IN LEARNING: It is the CFO's job to ask questions about any appropriation. More and more often, CFOs are developing and/or adopting new methodologies to assess the impact of learning on organizational financial performance. More than just determining return on investment where learning expenditures are concerned, CFOs are also beginning to include learning initiatives in their predictions of future financial performance. The enlightened CFO knows as well as anyone that the company that learns together earns together.

BACKGROUND: Many CFO's are certified public accountants and the holders of numerous degrees and certificates in finance or accounting. CFOs generally come out of accounting and finance backgrounds (although there are many exceptions). But without exception CFOs are good at gathering, organizing, processing, and reporting numbers.

COO (Chief Operating Officer)

DESCRIPTION: The CEO has the ultimate responsibility for *making it so*, but somebody really has to. The COO is the man or woman who oversees the organization's performance on a day-in and day-out basis. You could say that the CEO composes the symphony and the CFO audits ticket sales. But, the COO conducts the orchestra. The COO develops an operational strategy for the organization and then sees to it that the organization operates as effectively and efficiently as possible.

PRIMARY RESPONSIBILITIES

- Be the primary operational strategist
- Coordinate the harmonious interactivity of various departments and divisions
- Predict how internal and external forces might impact organizational efficiency
- Account for how sales, supply, and other factors will affect production
- See to it the organizational population is sufficiently motivated

- Guide the day-to-day activities of the organization so as to achieve organizational goals
- Keep a systemic perspective on how the organization operates, and update other executives
- Maintain an optimal balance between quality and efficiency

ROLE IN LEARNING: The link between a skilled and knowledgeable workforce and efficient operations is clear. The better prepared and informed people are, the better their contribution to operational excellence will be. Because learning activities have historically been seen as separate and distinct from operational activities, COOs must work closely with learning executives to make learning and operations almost indistinguishable.

BACKGROUND: COOs come from a variety of backgrounds including production management, quality and process control, engineering, finance and human resources. The most desirable quality in a COO is the ability to facilitate cooperation among various departments and interest groups. Like all chiefs, the COO must keep an eye toward organizational goals as s/he coordinates the efforts of many individuals.

CIO (Chief Information Officer)

DESCRIPTION: Computers are now indispensable. As organizations began to depend on computers not only to store and manipulate data, but also to generate revenue, somebody had to be in charge of them. And that somebody wasn't going to be the CEO, many of whom, especially in the 1970s and 80s couldn't operate a PC. (Some of the first computer classes were designed to demortify executives regarding computers.) The CIO was the first in the executive ranks to understand the magic boxes and supervise their use. Now they occupy every desktop.

PRIMARY RESPONSIBILITIES:

- Be the resident expert on computer technology
- Organize and operate computer centers
- Develop and maintain application systems

- Supervise local and wide area network operations
- Develop and implement strategies to make the most productive use of computer technologies
- Recommend information technology policies
- Develop procedures and standards for the use of computers in the workplace
- Define and assess information capability needs

ROLE IN LEARNING: As computers continue to be increasingly powerful tools in business, employees need to know how to operate both software and hardware. What employees don't know about computers can hurt the organization. The CIO must be a cheerleader for learning activities as well as a primary force in enabling all the variations on computer-based learning. The computer is becoming both the most significant singular reason for organizational learning as well as the most powerful tool in the course of learning activities. S/he who keeps the computers operating is vitally important to learning.

BACKGROUND: Requirements for the position of CIO often include a degree in computer science, an MBA, experience with advanced technologies (most of all the Internet), executive-level experience as a project director and IT manager, and demonstrated communication skills.

CTO (Chief Technology Officer)

DESCRIPTION: Rapid advances in computer technology and the emerging role of e-commerce began to weigh heavily upon the CIO. When the expanding universe of computer knowledge became too much for one position to handle, the CIO position divided like a cell. Typically, CIOs continued to engage in strategic planning and visioning as it involved computing while CTOs became the computing operatives.

PRIMARY RESPONSIBILITIES:

- Develop and maintain the organization's information technology and telecommunications infrastructure
- Advance the cause of the organization's information technology and telecommunications needs

- Stay abreast of the latest technological advancements and ensure that the organization remains technologically competitive
- Supervise the development and management of the organization's communications architecture
- Help senior management define technological objectives
- Research, evaluate, and disseminate information about new and existing technologies, products, and vendors that might impact the organization's position and/or products
- Speak and understand multiple software languages
- Support internal and external network operational needs

ROLE IN LEARNING: In much the same way that the world of the CIO represents both the need for learning and the tools for learning, the CTO must keep his or her finger on the pulse of an organization's level of technological expertise. The CTO must then assist the learning activities that address technical skill issues in any way s/he can. As technology continues to alter the way people learn, the CTO must help ensure that an organization's learning activities are technically current and sufficient.

BACKGROUND: Position requirements for CTOs often include extensive technology experience with an emphasis on data and text management, document management, e-publishing, office systems, Internet/Web, workflow, and application development. Other experience often called for includes eXtensible Markup Language (XML), Java, C++, COBRA, SGML, PC Docs, FileNet Saros, Documentum, and Lotus Doimino, among others.

CKO (Chief Knowledge Officer)

DESCRIPTION: When Peter Drucker coined the term "knowledge worker" in 1988 he acknowledged that the emphasis in business accomplishment had shifted from brawn to brains. The chief knowledge officer is responsible for ensuring that an organization maximizes the value it achieves through one of its most important assets—knowledge. The Center for research in Information Management at London Business School defines a CKO as, "A senior executive leading a knowledge management program or initiative and has the word 'knowledge' in his or her title." Some organizations use titles such as "Director of intellectual Capital" and "Director of Innovation" to describe the same function.

PRIMARY RESPONSIBILITIES:

- Gather competitive intelligence to stay on top of new developments in the industry and the marketplace

- Capture knowledge within the organization so that it can be shared and re-used

- Teach members of the organization about the knowledge resource centers available to them

- Serve as a catalyst for organizational change and invoke a more disciplined approach to decision-making

- Stop knowledge loss and leakage as people leave the organization

- Enhance creativity and innovation through an overall framework of knowledge management

- Help repeat successes and share best practices

- Facilitate connections, coordination, and communications

ROLE IN LEARNING: The role of a chief knowledge officer falls into two broad areas: current awareness and data warehousing. Moreover, the CKO manages institutional learning on a minute-by-minute and year-by-year basis. The CKO must articulate the knowledge agenda and actively promote and justify it, often in the face of cynicism or open hostility.

BACKGROUND: CKOs come from diverse backgrounds including finance, legal, marketing, HR, IT, consulting, and communications. The CKO shouldn't necessarily be a product of one discipline. The more balanced the background among various disciplines, the more suitable the candidate for CKO. More than any other single factor, the CKO needs to be zealous about knowledge and contributing a truly competitive advantage to the organization.

CLO (Chief Learning Officer)

DESCRIPTION: According to the Corporate University Exchange in New York, the CLO is the "new strategic head of corporate education and training departments." CUX also reports that the CLO is increasingly on political par with the CFO and CIO. The average CLO (as reported by CUX) earned $134,550 in 1999. Often, the CLO's compensation package is tied to performance measures that include personal performance, organizational success, and the efficient use corporate learning budgets.

PRIMARY RESPONSIBILITIES:

- Develop a vision for learning as it contributes to organizational success
- Develop a strategy to make formal and informal learning a part of daily organizational life
- Champion the cause of learning to all stakeholders
- Help calculate the direct and indirect value of learning for internal and external enlightenment
- Translate articulated organizational outcomes into learning activities and processes
- Build alliances between those who have valuable knowledge and those who can benefit from it
- Bring technology to bear on organizational learning needs
- Build and sustain an infrastructure for organizational learning

ROLE IN LEARNING: The CLO is more directly responsible for formal and informal learning activities than any other executive. Generally speaking, the CLO leverages learning to support organizational strategies and tactics. Where there are corporate universities and CLOs in the same organization, the CLO will almost invariably be in charge of the university. In all cases it is vitally important that the

CLO be able to unify business realities with educational aspirations.

BACKGROUND: Like the CKO, the CLO often has an eclectic background. Some key qualities in a CLO are partnership, collaboration, and communication. It is not uncommon to find that CLOs have backgrounds and degrees in education (particularly corporate education), business administration, and HR. However, the most effective CLOs are frequently those with hands-on experience running business units because s/he must be a real contributor to the achievement of organizational goals, not merely a learning enthusiast. There are a number of graduate programs in universities which offer special opportunity for emerging CLOs,

CPO (Chief People Officer)

DESCRIPTION: As the importance of intellectual capital continues to grow, organizational leaders are looking at their human assets more and more holistically. As enlightened and informed business leaders have known for a long time, there is no absolute wall or barrier between an individuals personal and professional life. Things that affect individuals on a personal level, such as family and personal needs, have a tremendous impact on their professional performance. The position of CPO is the way that some organizational leaders are attempting to address the personal and professional needs of employees in order to increase job satisfaction, performance, loyalty, and professional development.

PRIMARY RESPONSIBILITIES:

- Ensure the satisfaction of the organizational population
- Design and deploy methods to monitor satisfaction
- Keep the goals of the organization aligned as closely as possible with the personal goals of the employees
- Make sure that employees have mobility and opportunity in professional development
- Provide access to whatever services employees need to

minimize distractions and increase focus on job-related activities

- Diagnose the causes of poor performance and address them as they relate to employee satisfaction

- Maximize the contributions made by the organization to the comfort and loyalty of each employee

- Champion the importance of employee satisfaction to executives who might otherwise be more focused on financial performance and productivity

ROLE IN LEARNING: The CPO must be an avid supporter of all the CLO and CKO do in the cause of the learning organization. More than that, the CPO must advise the CLO and CKO regarding the role that learning and communications play in employee satisfaction. Usually, the CPO will be in charge of all HR functions, including compensation.

BACKGROUND: CPOs most often emerge from the ranks of HR professionals and sometimes have degrees in social work and psychology. CPOs must be well-balanced in their appreciation of the organization's overarching needs and the satisfaction coefficient of the employees. CPOs need to understand what drives and sustains top executives as well as other employees.

What's in a Name?

In addition to those previously described, even more titles have appeared in organizational life, such as CCOs (chief communications officers) and CMOs (chief marketing officers). Many times the latest organizational acronyms are little more than new monikers for old positions such as CLO (training executives) and CPO (HR executives). Sometimes, however, these changes signal trends in organizational direction.

Higher value is now being placed on communications, marketing, organizational learning, and human resource functions. It naturally follows that increasing recognition and regard for human capital, inside and outside of the organization is leading to more attention being paid to these roles. In many ways all of these issues, learning, satisfaction, information, technology, communications, internal and external marketing, need to be part of everyone's daily routine if an organization is going to be both healthy and competitive.

The CTO grew out of the world of the CIO; the CKO is now leading the way to the CLO. Recognizing that much of the learning and exchange of information in organizations takes place outside of formal learning activities, organizational designers came up with the CKO to get a handle on the wealth of knowledge within their organizations. Even though they are separate designations for distinct functions, the CKO and CLO are probably the most overlapping roles and responsibilities. The CPO is never far away from the same human capital issues that CKOs and CLOs are concerned with, but the CPO has a more human resource orientation. Communications is the river that runs through the organization. In short, we will preserve the distinctions as much as possible as we discuss broad-reaching issues that impact everyone dedicated to organizational excellence.

Keep the Conversation Going

Informal learning and information sharing takes place constantly. Conversations around the water cooler or while waiting in line the cafeteria can, and often do, affect the performance of individuals and groups of individuals throughout your organization. Anyone involved with learning and knowledge is committed to keeping the conversation going on whatever level it is occurring. This means that CKOs, CLOs, and CPOs must all consciously consider organizational development issues such as organizational culture, design, and excellence.

People within any given organization, develop collective ways of thinking whether it is consciously guided or not. The continuous conversation throughout an organization reflects the collective thinking, be it good or bad. All executives, especially CKOs, CLOs, and CPOs, must be committed to actively participating in the conversation and guiding it toward organizational goals. And, the only way to manage the corporate conversation, since most of it takes place outside of organized activities, is to stay ahead of it. Formulating and carrying out strategies and policies to keep people challenged, motivated, and focused are infinitely more valuable than after-the-fact downsizing and damage control.

To varying degrees, all of the chiefs, led by the CKO, CLO, and/or CPO must work in concert to recognize learning as a critical business strategy, not a luxury. They must all work together to create and sustain an environment that acknowledges the collective intelligence of the organization. Finally, everyone, not merely the CKO and CLO, must work to embed and integrate learning in all business processes.

From the top down all chiefs must endeavor to:

- Maximize the returns on investments in knowledge—people, processes, and intellectual capital
- Exploit intangible assets such as know-how, patents, and customer relationships
- Repeat successes and share best practices
- Improve innovation in the organization and commercialize ideas
- Avoid knowledge loss and leakage after organizational restructuring
- Maintain competitive market position or advantage
- Work toward improved employee performance
- Facilitate the concept of the learning organization

The CLO is Stepping Forward

The Reengineering Resource Center concept applied and helped popularize the term Chief Learning Officer to describe the types of knowledge management that were on the horizon and dedicated to creating what is becoming known as *the learning organization.* In many cases, *"The new CLO is in charge of the corporation's collective thinking. He or she is responsible for maximizing the organization's intelligence and commitment,"* says Joel Yanowitz of Innovation Associates in Boston. *"One of the primary jobs of the CLO is to identify the variety of hidden organizational mental models so that they can be aligned with the corporate vision."* Daniel Kim of MIT's Sloan School of Management adds, *"If mental models, those mindsets, frames of reference, and value structures that we all use to view 'reality' are not explicit and shared, then information and knowledge pass [us by and don't connect]."*

As noted earlier, the term Chief Learning Officer grew from the talk about learning organizations. The goals and aspirations were, and are, similar to current organizational attitudes regarding intellectual equity. Peter Senge, a leader in the learning organization movement, argues that, *"Learning organizations are not only adaptive, which is to cope, but generative, which is to create."* According to Dave Ulrich of the University of Michigan and Hope Greenfield from Digital Equipment Corporation, the movement toward making learning a part of doing business instead of a distraction or disruption calls for some new approaches:

- Move from generic classroom training to tailored competence-based, Web and media access training
- Use both case studies and action learning
- Focus on both individual competence to organizational capabilities
- Facilitate both individual and team participation
- Transition from classroom to overall (ubiquitous) learning
- Engage in both competence-based classes to strategy-based courses
- Move from external to internal presenters with customized materials
- Include both bounded to unbounded training sessions
- Foster an understanding of value chain participation
- Understand both local to global learning models
- Foster performance improvement as a way of work life

Characteristics of Learning, Knowledge, and People Executives

Good leaders have always done what we look to a CKO/CLO/CPO to do now. Nobody told them, they just somehow understood the value of people. Such leaders have, however, been rare. In today's increasingly knowledge-driven marketplace, organizational executives no longer have the luxury of burning and turning talent. It is a seller's market for workers who are willing to learn. Here are some questions and answers for those who want to get deep into the concept of organizational knowledge and learning.

Question: How does a CKO/CLO/CPO think?

Answer: Strategic and conceptual thinkers make good CKOs/CLOs/CPOs because they never lose sight of the context and perspective in which they are operating. They are big picture thinkers who view knowledge as a tool and resource to execute the organization's strategy in the environment in which it operates.

Question: Does a CKO/CLO/CPO need to be a good communicator?

Answer: A CKO/CLO/CPO needs to be an exceptional communicator. A CKO/CLO/CPO must be an active listener, able to pick up on subtle and often unspoken messages that effect the organization and the individuals working within it. The CKO/CLO/CPO is not only someone who communicates very well; she or he must be able to facilitate communication among others. Setting up information sharing networks is a good example. Whenever possible, a CKO/CLO/CPO sets the communications agenda, keeping a close eye on organizational issues and the desired outcomes of organizational opportunities.

Question: What is effective communication?

Answer: Communication is the process of encoding information and transmitting it to someone else who then decodes the information. Verbal, non-verbal, or encrypted, communications all involve the same process. Only the *method* of coding and decoding changes. Effective communication takes place when behavior is influenced by the message. Effective communication causes something to happen, which might mean causing something not to change for the moment.

Question: Is the CKO/CLO a leader?

Answer: Quality leadership skills are part and parcel of any alphabet executive's professional life. A person can't ethically be interested in what people have in their heads if she or he is not genuinely interested in the people themselves. That's why CKO/CLO responsibilities are frequently almost indistinguishable from the Chief People Officer in some firms. Morale and motivation are important considerations to any CKO who wants to make a substantial contribution to the success of his or her employer. And the CKO's activities have a tremendous impact on organizational behaviors and attitudes. An organization's culture is rooted in the hearts and minds of its staff. Employees' hearts and minds are within the CKO/CLO/CPOs' domain.

Question: Does the CKO/CLO/CPO need to be a top-level executive?

Answer: Absolutely. The CKO/CLO/CPO must have the authority to champion causes that aren't always popular, especially among older autocrats and habitual bean counters that lack the vision to see the larger goals. The CKO/CLO/CPO must have sufficient power to keep critical projects alive and protect knowledge initiatives through the long haul. Having said all of that, we realize that anyone at such a top level needs to be a diplomat to one degree or another. The CKO/CLO/CPO needs to know how to get along in order to be an effective advocate for his or her knowledge agenda. When it is time to defend an activity, the CKO/CLO/CPO must be an able defender, even in the face of criticism and hostility, particularly from those who don't ever seem to get it.

Question: What do CKOs and CLOs think about all day long?

Answer: Chief knowledge and officers think about knowledge and they think about learning. They contemplate the vastness of the knowledge inside and outside of the organization and do their best to frame it in the context of organizational success--success for the whole as well as the individual. They also think about who possesses the knowledge. They ponder what knowledge is going to be most critical to the organization and how it be disseminated quickly with maximum benefit. CKOs/CLOs constantly monitor organizational life and performance. The ask themselves how well managers are managing in light of available information, and, in which sectors of the organization are non-responsive to knowledge resources or resisting them altogether?

Question: Can CKOs/CLOs/CPOs remain objective?

Answer: CKOs/CLOs/CPOs must be vigilant about their own reality. The CKO/CLO/CPO must self-assess if he or she is getting jaded or burned out.

Question: Are there others inside or outside of the organization who can help keep the CKO/CLO on track and in balance?

Answer: Among the most important recurring questions to a good CKO/CLO/CPO are *"what actions and behaviors are resulting from the knowledge/learning/HR program?" "Are the knowledge/learning/HR resources hitting the bottom line as well as they should?"* CKOs/CLOs/CPOs do a lot of asking and a lot of listening.

From CIO to CKO

In 1999 the General Services Administration of the Federal Government adopted the position of chief knowledge officer calling it *"an executive management post that will be responsible for tapping the agency's information technology to help employees access information for their jobs."* Who did the GSA tap for the new CKO position? The old CIO. For some, the line of distinction is still hard to see, but at the GSA, there is now a CIO, CKO, *and* a chief people officer.

It is bound to get confusing where the three job descriptions overlap. However, the agency describes the CKO's function as leading the agency's use of knowledge management practices, which include gathering, sorting, and presenting information throughout the organization in a way that makes it easier for people to understand and share information and use it to make decisions. The CKO/CLO/CPO will work closely. The CIO will align information technology investments with business goals. The CPO will make sure the organization has the right people to perform its mission. The CKO will use information technology to share knowledge among workers and to increase workers' knowledge.

A 2000 study of local, state, and federal agency CIOs indicated, among other things, that public agencies are most focused on developing network infrastructure. According to the CIOs, connectivity and information networking are by far the most important uses of advanced computer technologies. They're not hot on the idea of outsourcing solutions for information analysis, learning, etc. They feel technologies' most critical applications are the ability to send information to *each other*. Perhaps this is why the clerical layer of government is shrinking. Computer networks now enable government middle managers to transmit information without going through multiple layers of clerk typists. Computers are taking over many left-brain functions to fuel up managers and innovative thinkers to exercise and pump up their right-brain creativity.

The public sector move to CKOs comes at a time when research still indicates that government is making little use of business intelligence tools. Like their private sector counterparts, the CKO initiative at the General Services Administration was established to encourage creativity among employees and to promote practices that help foster change. The agency is also creating an online repository on its website that will centralize how-to information for employees, such as how to apply for federal health insurance and how to help federal contractors get on the GSA schedule. Like many private sector Websites, the GSA site will include contact information for all GSA programs and offices.

Many of the CKO's duties at the GSA resemble what we customarily expect from a CIO. The difference is in the CKO's focus. FutureNext is an eBusiness and supply chain-consulting firm that looks to its CKO to *"manage our knowledge and experience as carefully as we manage our financial and other key corporate assets. Our intellectual capital is a key advantage we bring to our clients."* The credo at FutureNext is that success with knowledge management requires an overall program that addresses three key elements:

1. Alignment with business processes to deliver bottom line benefits to business

2. A focus on the cultural aspects of knowledge management to foster a collaborative knowledge sharing culture

3. Support of enabling technologies that provide tools for collaboration and enable the collection and sharing of information and knowledge throughout the organization

In additional to increasing creativity and fostering change, other benefits of knowledge management practices include:

- Lowering costs
- Improving the quality of the work
- Facilitating connections and coordinating communications
- Executing business processes faster, more effectively and efficiently
- Developing an overall framework that guides knowledge management
- Overseeing the development of hard and soft knowledge infrastructure
- Promoting the knowledge agenda inside and outside of the organization

CKO Opens Intranet

One of the first orders of business for the GSA's CKO was to establish a corporate information network, or Intranet, to improve information sharing among its fourteen thousand employees and their customers. In the private sector, Carol Bothwell, CKO for Computer Sciences Corporation, is in charge of CSC Sources, an enterprise-wide environment that enables CSC to build and leverage its knowledge, experience, and expertise on a global basis. With fifty-four thousand employees and seven hundred offices worldwide, that's quite an Intranet. As CKO, Bothwell is responsible for designing CSC's knowledge strategy and is in charge of managing CSC's knowledge program that provides the services necessary to maintain and evolve CSC Sources and CSC Catalysts, the company's core business methodology.

CKO/CLO/CPO as a Strategy

More than a mere title or vague concept, the chief officers of knowledge, learning, and people need to be action-oriented and part of a larger plan. Strategy Software, Inc. has begun development of digital aids to help transform the CKO from idea to strategy. In developing what they call Competitive Intelligence Information Tracking, Strategy Software asked CKOs and CLOs what they felt were among their most important contributions to their organizations. Here are some of the most frequent answers:

- Facilitate creation of knowledge-building processes
- Make knowledge permanent by capturing and retaining key information learned by employees and turning it into company knowledge
- Make knowledge readily available through structured databases and indexed document management systems
- Foster the use and reuse of previously-acquired knowledge
- Reduce wasted time and effort researching information that already exists
- Understand that the 80-20 rule (where 20% of the people do 80% of the work) is really more like 99-1 when it comes to knowledge

We see all of these efforts as attempts to turn knowledge and information into ammunition in the battle for competitive supremacy. Organizations regularly report that they are upping the stakes on knowledge sharing in order to increase productivity. CKOs necessarily have knowledge of and, hopefully, some experience in information technology, business renewal, communications, teamwork, process management, change management, and human and organizational development as well as various forms of learning initiatives.

The CKO/CLO and Organizational Learning

> *"We know that people just don't have time to sit in the classroom for five days anymore. That's not today's model of learning. It's better to learn something just when you need it, and take what you've learned and apply it to what you're doing. Technology is going to be a great tool for that kind of learning."*
>
> —Shereen Remez,
> CKO, General Services Administration

CKOs/CLOs/CPOs must champion the cause of learning in the organization and ensure that the right people get the right information at the right time. In most organizations with CKOs/CLOs/CPOs all three are in charge of at least some of the formal learning. Even if that's not always the case learning is inherent in the CKO's/CLO's/CPO's duties. Anything CKOs/CLOs/CPOs do in the course of acting on their job descriptions causes learning to occur, whether there is another executive in charge of formal organizational learning or not. Much of the learning that results from CKO activities is the ubiquitous, continuous kind. It is impossible to fully assess in advance what someone is going to do with shared information. It is hard to predict when an unplanned light bulb will suddenly go on inside someone's head, or when someone will suddenly connect the dots that nobody knew were there to begin with. The learning that the CKO deals with may be minute-by-minute, year-by-year, and all at once.

The CKO/CLO/CPO as Organizational Designers

Poor organizational design and structure can slow

down or stop the progress that conventional wisdom says ought to be happening. Sometimes it is the timidity of the leadership. Whatever the case, organizations rarely come to a grinding halt even as a lot of people know what's happening. They just weren't listened to soon enough, if at all. Additionally, we are assuming that they haven't become so cynical over time that they just watch their own enterprise go belly-up for lack of any sense of ownership. When the knowledge that people possess is mined and acknowledged, their sense of ownership expands. People want their leaders to be aware of what they can contribute. The CKO/CLO/CPO needs to design and install techniques and processes to create, protect, and use knowledge, learning, and satisfaction to promote organizational goals.

We are not all created equal, and all intellectual assets are not the same. Patents and inventions are traditionally protected. But what about proprietary work processes and procedures? They need to be protected as well, if nothing more than recording them to keep the stores of knowledge up to date. Establishing a reward system for sharing information indicates the organization's commitment to acknowledging what workers know and learn. CKOs/CLOs/CPOs make sure that individuals who make intellectual contributions see the impact their contributions make on the success of the organization. This is particularly true if the source of the knowledge is far away from the executive suite. The CKO/CLO/CPO must continually articulate the value and purpose of stored and shared knowledge. They must also see to it that people are rewarded for sharing and prudently reusing knowledge.

A Final Challenge for the CKO/CLO/CPO

The greatest challenge for most CKOs/CLOs/CPOs in knowledge and learning management programs is in dealing with organizational culture. Most groups haven't been organized around knowledge, learning, and satisfaction as primary resources and therefore tend to reject new initiatives like a body sometimes rejects a transplanted organ. This is true on a macro level where leaders do not particularly want to deal with a changing organization. It is also true at a micro level where individual workers have a routine going and they're not anxious to change it. The most sophisticated and advanced IT tools will be of little use to members of an organization who don't want to or don't know how to communicate with one another.

The seven key challenges of CKOs/CLOs/CPOs are to:

1. Design human and information systems that make information available, and link community members together and encourage interaction

2. Develop communities that share knowledge while maintaining an open atmosphere that promotes diversity and encourages new and extraordinary thinking

3. Create an environment that truly values the sharing of knowledge

4. Help employees to be open to the ideas of others, willing to share ideas unselfishly, and maintain a thirst for new knowledge

5. Facilitate the learning environment by helping people to learn how to learn

6. Encourage choices, options and access to performance improvement learning

7. Champion the learning organization

At the end of the day the CKO/CLO/CPO will have helped move his or her organization significantly farther down the road to success and fulfillment than it would have traveled without him or her. There is a great deal of fermentation going on as CKO/CLO/CPO positions continue to emerge. How the concepts themselves evolve over time has yet to be seen. Most relevant now, are the emerging initiatives involving organizational intelligence and the increasing importance of the issues the alphabet executives represent. We believe that when all is said and done *learning* will spell the difference between success and failure for the individual as well as the organization.

Where are we going now?

This is a clear trend now toward an increasing number of CLOs, including CLO organizations. Learning and learning how to learn is the next step beyond sharing knowledge and information. All of the chiefs are "solutions architects." And, solutions architecture represents an overarching concept central to the changing roles of all of the chiefs. The CLO role in a company makes a statement.

As the importance of e-learning opportunities rise in corporate culture, as training methods involve greater understanding and use of technique, the importance of the learning officer responsibility inside the organization is visibly increasing in importance. So, there is a clear leadership trend embodied by "the emerging chiefs." "Chiefs as champions" offers a leadership model. "Hail to the CLO".

In addition, new degree programs such as the Ph.D. or Ed.D. in Psychology, Education, and Media Studies, such as those at the Fielding Graduate Institute (fielding.edu) where I teach, are opening the way for mid career professional adults to pursue their educational programs as Scholar/Practitioners. This new type of program is flexible, serves the individuals own objectives, and is not bound by time and place. It is more in the European model of Oxford and Cambridge.

Solutions Architect is a term applied to many emerging roles. Solutions architects offer blueprints for progress. As the corporate university is growing in stature and importance, so is the role of the chiefs, and especially the Chief Learning Officer as a leader for the emerging learning organizations. "Hail to the chiefs."

Ivy-Covered Clicks
The Ups and Downs of E-Learning in Higher and Adult Education

In the print-centric world of the twentieth century, the primary method for information sharing was ink and paper. Photography, telephony, radio, film, audio recording, and video recording each found a place, and each of these new wonders had its own unique communications strengths and weaknesses. For most of the twentieth century, each of these technologies was still essentially a separate medium. Film and video brought still images to life, sound enhanced them, but paper continued to dominate as the preferred medium for distributing the written word and images.

The mantra entering the twenty-first century has been called "convergence." Television brings new and more exciting learning experiences into the classroom, but coordinated audio and visual learning systems, including telecourses, are still in their infancy. Although Sesame Street, The Electric Company, and other educational producers and programs continuously improved the content and quality of educational programming through the 1990s, there was no overpowering, pervasive, technology to transcend distance and enable direct interaction between teacher and student outside the traditional classroom—until now.

What educational television did was couple onto the cultural transformation that was taking place through the picture tube. Everyone born after World War II is now considered part of what is called the "television generation." Today we are approaching the forth generation of those who have been exposed to television almost from birth. Long before they start school, most children in the world know how to watch television.

With the growing sophistication of television viewers everywhere, producers of educational television have learned that programming must have production values comparable to those of mainstream movies and television programming if young audiences are expected to pay attention.

Many pundits now say that the biggest barrier to the overall success of early electronic educational media was the difficulty of students and instructors to interact effectively—both with the media and each other. Over the decades, the obstacles to media-assisted learning were recognized and advances were made to smooth the bumps along the path. In the 1970s Coastline Community College in Orange County, California, was the recognized leader in broadcast courses for academic credit. Understanding that telecourse students, like their traditional classroom counterparts, often need direct contact with the teacher, CCC bought fifteen answering machines to record messages from telecourse students to their instructors. The instructors replied to the students' calls within a day or so, which was then considered a revolutionary response time. The professional-grade answering machines cost nearly $1,000 each, representing a major investment for a college in the 1970s. Despite the high cost, this answering machine/ telecourse combination became a standard in telecourse design. That was the best state-of-the-art interactive technology could offer at the time. Today, CCC is an acknowledged pioneer in distance learning and, through continuing innovation, remains a model for distance education along with other leaders like The Tele Learning People, Intelecom, Dallas Community College District,

Miami Community College, Miracopa Community College District, and the League for Innovation.

It is easy to forget that television was once considered revolutionary technology. Television has proved to be the world's most influential electronic medium with respect to both individual and societal human behavior and remains a powerful tool for education. It will retain significant power in its many new iterations. TV has been an informal education tool that can teach or alter human behavior without learners becoming consciously involved and precisely for that reason, advertisers spend billions of dollars every year to distribute their messages. Informal learning often takes place most effectively when the participant is actively involved. Television can be described as "lean back" while the computer is best described as "lean forward." Learning may occur in either case.

Just as children raised on television are conditioned to learn from the moving pictures and sounds they see and hear, new generations are growing up in front of PCs and TVPCs. The computer is technically more suited to formal teaching with the learner more likely to be actively involved. Formal teaching involves students who are consciously engaged in learning. Subjects ranging from needlework to nuclear science can now be effectively taught online thanks to the interactive capabilities and data storage capacities of computers. But, the learner has to *want* to learn, and the process of conscious learning embodies both skills and habits.

The evolution of television has been simpler to observe than the evolution of the microprocessor with its constant, rapid changes that dramatically alter it with each new technological advance. The advent of digital technology brought about the convergence of many communications media, the catalyst being the microprocessor that emerged from the digital processing (dp) chip in the mid 1980s. Through microprocessors, computers and television screens have led us into a PCTV, TVPC, split-screen, two-screen world. Although it wasn't developed primarily as a learning tool, the computer, like TV, can be a formidable tool for education. With the ability to link together locally and globally, computer-centric education is rising to new levels.

The Revolving Door

Let's fast-forward a little to the year 2012 and picture a student sitting in an elementary school classroom. The teacher decides that the class needs to watch a video with computer-animated graphics depicting the metamorphosis of a caterpillar into a butterfly. She overrides the high definition computer screen that forms the surface of every student's desk. As the students watch the digitized program they click on the moments of the program that they want to bookmark to later remind themselves of questions to ask in the class discussion to follow.

After a lively discussion (in case you are wondering, teachers will always be central to learning) the students are assigned an essay on the metamorphosis each has just watched. As they compose their essays, in class, on their desk/computers, the teacher monitors their progress on her master computer, sending electronic notes to individual students as they write. Before the compositions are finished the teacher knows who has a solid grasp on metamorphosis and who does not

The immediate application of new information increases retention. In earlier times, students would learn lessons and input data into their minds, often struggling to retrieve it weeks, months or years later when it was needed. With today's technology, refined and reinvented tomorrow, learning may become synchronous with each learner's mental pulse, psychological learning profile, and physiological cycles.

In the future workplace, similar innovations are taking place. Engineers reference necessary data online simultaneously with creating their designs. Architects study historical renderings and current data at the same time they draft plans for new structures. Physicians can access stored patient data or view visual playbacks of previous operations as they conduct surgery, while the patient's vital signs and other critical information are displayed in the operating theater *and* in an attending surgeon's office half-way around the world, giving physicians broad, virtual access to collaboration and the expertise of subspecialists around the world in a cost-effective manner.

The possibilities are only limited by your imagination. The seeds of things to come are already planted and the new growth is beginning to sprout in technological and corporate education trends.

E-Learning Defined

As Mark Twain amusingly said, "Don't let school interfere with your education." Writing for INTERNETWEEK John Berry exclaimed, "Training is dead—long live e-learning." Elliott Maise, founder of the Maise Center, wrote that "e-learning is a wider tent than just online learning, Web-based training, CBT, technology assisted, distance learning or other phrases." Maise's point is that e-learning is about more than the technology involved. I add that it is about the "experience of learning in this new age." Each of these quotes reflects some truth.

E-learning is an evolving phenomena of the changing classroom. It is a formal educational process that alters or extends the traditional classroom, providing a new, distributed opportunity for learning that can occur without the barriers of time or place. There are two key differences between traditional education and e-learning. E-learning improves flexibility and access regardless of time, place or *pace of learning*. It also reaches out to non-traditional students who must fit their studies around workplace and family responsibilities, geographical barriers, or personal challenges.

Instruction over distance is delivered using a number of technologies depending on which is most appropriate for the subject and the student. Preferred technologies may be as straightforward as the classic correspondence-school model of paper-based and postal-delivered instruction. Audio technologies, such as tape, telephone conference calls, or radio allow synchronous delivery of instruction to a virtual group of students. Video technology, such as videotape, compressed video, cable, or satellite-delivered programming adds more flexibility and sophistication to instructional design. Each modality has its appropriate, effective place.

Computer-based learning technologies such as CD-ROM and Web-connected DVD-ROM, the Internet, and desktop videoconferencing make tailoring individual instruction efficient and effective. Support technologies such as e-mail, fax, telephone, PDAs, and the Web facilitate communication and interactivity, even in totally synchronous delivery systems. More specifically, e-learning is connected learning. Learners may be connected online to the instructor, connected online to one another, connected to their instructional and research resources, or all of the above.

Corporate Learning

Corporate learning has been broadly defined as any "enhancement to an employee's skills in the classroom by an instructor." We now recognize that employees acquire knowledge and build skills in a wide variety of formal and informal activities. Classroom training is often delivered "just-in-case," while e-learning, via the Web or CD-ROM, may be delivered "just-in-time."

Learning and Earning

One of the most powerful drivers of workplace learning is change. E-learning is essential to keep pace with the emerging global e-culture, so it follows that commerce and business have a vested interest in improving the quality of workplace education. For many enterprises e-learning spells the difference between dot-com and dot-bomb. Rapidly changing workplace applications of new technology alter the job functions of employees and without keeping up, failure is imminent. Ironically, enormous investments in new technological applications often yield disappointingly low returns because employees do not receive proper training to effectively harness the power of these systems. E-learning can deliver learning experiences on the same technological platform that employees will use on the job.

Examples

Corning, Inc. used Internet-based learning to teach 70,000 employees in seventy countries as it implemented a new Enterprise Resource Planning system (ERP). Corning's director of information technology, Steve Cooper, estimates that the company saved between $2 million and $3 million using online learning techniques for that single application alone and Sun Microsystems turned to a Web-based solution to bring 7,500 employees up to speed on a new Oracle application in just two weeks.

Mice in the Ivy-covered Halls

The traditional scenario in higher education typically has the eighteen-year-old student relocating to the institution. Now, education is no further away than the student's fingertips, night or day. Even as enrollment in colleges and universities is at an all-time high, online learning is exploding onto the scene. Some defenders of traditional schooling remain threatened and leery of the new opportunities of e-learning. This ongoing scuffle between traditionalists and progressive educators has kicked up enough dirt to expose the long-buried (but not forgotten) tension and distrust between the private sector and the public sector. However, both groups are gaining experience, and accruing leadership as the presence of media in the classroom and the workplace quickly increases and becomes more successful.

Some traditional educators see the emerging for-profit training and education programs, especially online, as an attempt to muscle in on turf that has always belonged to established colleges and universities. For-profit, commercial-education ventures such as the University of Phoenix Online, Jones International University (the first completely Web-based university to receive accreditation), Unext, Quisic, and eCollege have addressed the trend toward online learning by repackaging or reproducing courses taught at established universities. George Washington University is already generating revenue from a courseware system developed within the university called Prometheus.

Vanderbilt University was among the first institutions other than George Washington to license Prometheus, followed by Stanford University, the University of Chicago and others. Cyber-educators envision a new world of opportunity with education set free from the confines of the classroom. In 1999, more than one million individuals in the Unites States took courses online and that same year the first three masters degree candidates at Jones International University graduated online.

Learn Ware International is a good example of another current trend. Learn Ware is a privately held, for-profit firm based in Baltimore that is a licensee of Johns Hopkins University. The unique relationship with the university allows Learn Ware to display the marks and seals of the university, which enhance its credibility for sales and marketing purposes and give it a distinct competitive advantage.

Until recently, most academics would call a partnership between an institution of higher learning and a for-profit entrepreneurial enterprise a pact with the devil. Johns Hopkins is not alone in the tradition-meets-innovation trend. Other universities with ties to for-profit online educational enterprises or, in some cases, their own for-profit subsidiaries, include the University of Chicago, NYU, Stanford, Wharton, Cornell, and Columbia. In addition, Eastern Michigan University, Vanderbilt, The University of Southern California, Walden University, The University of Maryland, and The American Film Institute also have such programs.

For some university systems, going online is more than a matter of serving working adults and alumni; it is a matter of survival. Millions of members of "Generation Y" are expected to flood university campuses over the next ten years. Dr. Charles B. Reed, chancellor of the California State University system, feels that physical campuses will be inadequate to meet the tidal wave of new students. Applications to state colleges are expected to increase 20 percent by 2008. Serving a portion of new students with online technology is necessary.

Online recruitment is also a major activity for universities attempting to attract the best quality applicants for admissions. Now, online programs and services for alumni represent a potentially lucrative business opportunity, with all types of learning partnerships with for-profit, online enterprises in the middle. Technology offers new ways to expand educational programs for alumni while, requiring institutional leaders to consider creative relationships with allies and audiences. "The trick is to find synergies that will make technology serve educational goals without bankrupting [the school] in the process."

Partnerships between universities and commercial education firms seem to minimize the threat of bankruptcy. One example is the University of California, San Diego, which has partnered with INTERVU Inc. of San Diego and Intel Corp. of Santa Clara, California, to launch a Web site featuring broadcast programming that will draw on the intellectual, scientific, and artistic talent of the University of California campuses.

Despite the fact that the increasing need for knowledge (as indicated by how much employers are willing to pay for it), is putting a strain on ivy-covered walls, traditional colleges and universities everywhere, along with their private-sector counterparts, are setting up their own online learning opportunities. The factor which will determine success in the future is relevance.

Even if there were enough chairs, desks, and instructors to handle every person seeking advanced education, traditional schools could not demonstrate the flexibility, timeliness, and overall relevance that are the trademarks of online education and other distance-learning devices including CD-ROM and DVD. GlobalLearningSystems and Panasonic are melding technologies to provide i-DVD, a new technology that sidestep bandwidth issues by leveraging the advantages of both the Internet and DVDs. The Web-enabled DVD, print-on-demand, PDAs employing "learning to go" concepts and all manner of new strategies are emerging which build and maintain skills.

"Educators, content providers, policymakers, and the high-tech industry have been partnering for more than two decades to bring the benefits of computer technology to the classroom. While the integration of technology as a teaching tool has been a gradual process, learners of all ages are reaping benefits at an exponential rate due to the increasing ubiquity of the Internet."

Existing colleges and universities are not closing their doors; their own graduates are going online to become more competitive in the corporate world, and they are doing it from computer terminals and workstations in their offices and/or homes.

Students in record numbers will continue to travel to college and university campuses everywhere. At the same time, knowledge and information are traveling wherever they are needed, whenever they are needed, via the Internet and other new techniques. The proliferation of media has opened new doors and channels to bring knowledge and information to hungry learners around the world.

Bricks and Mortar or Brand Name

Over the years, an MBA from a recognized university has been a respected credential for students entering the work force for the first time, as well as mid-career learners. As we just mentioned, traditional degrees and credentials and new degrees and certifications aren't necessarily mutually exclusive. New types of credentials such as Certified Systems Engineer (CSE), Certified Systems Developer (CSD), and Certified Internet Specialist (CIS), and as we move deeper into the digital era, certifications from names such as Cisco, Learning Tree, Lotus, Microsoft, Novell, and others will carry as much, or even more, importance in the workplace as traditional degrees.

An accredited MBA generally warrants a certain level of compensation. In today's environment, that same MBA will qualify an individual for substantially higher compensation if s/he *also* has a Cisco or Microsoft certification. This is the result of application-specific knowledge and training increasing in value as business is conducted in a technically specific manner. The bricks and mortar degrees, as always, are the stadium. Applications or vendor-specific certifications are the technical skills necessary to play the game once you, a player, steps onto the field.

Anticipation and Response

The digital technology that is the foundation of e-learning designs opens up vast new possibilities for anticipating issues and responding to them. A worker's compliance with corporate learning requirements and electives can be tracked. As e-learners participate in and complete courses, instructors and knowledge executives may view areas of strength and weakness and, through digital technology, help strategic planners to anticipate performance issues and plan accordingly. If extra individualized instruction is required, courseware can be designed to meet the immediate and long-term needs of the worker.

Bricks and Clicks

Thomas Weisel of Thomas Weisel Partners, a merchant banking firm, calls business-to-business e*Learning solutions *"an emerging $11.4 billion opportunity."* Established universities have realized that they can use online courses to expand their enrollment (and tuition revenue) without expanding their physical plant.

Fairleigh Dickinson University, with an enrollment of 9,000, now requires students to take at least one course per year online. "We believe it's a transforming learning tool," says Professor J. Michael Adams. "If we are preparing global citizens, we believe that our graduates must be facile with the Internet." Students can choose from over a dozen online courses in English literature, global issues, and even the Internet itself. Over the next four years the university expects to expand its online catalogue to over sixty courses.

University faculty members can also expand their earning ability without taking on more classroom obligations. They can teach online, especially in self-paced online courses where student work and faculty responses are not delivered in real time. Thanks to the Internet, an American education has become a possibility for many students from other countries. (It has also attracted non-domestic tuition that American universities would not have received in the past.) On a humanitarian level, the best thing for developing nations is to better educate their populations, and the Internet is playing a key role in that effort.

Capital investment in private education and training companies has never been higher, especially investment in those organizations that do business primarily over the Internet. A quote repeatedly made by Chief Executive Officer of Cisco Systems, John Chambers, predicts *"E-learning is the next trend after e-commerce. It's the next killer application on the Internet."*

Courses are not the only things available on line. Certificates, A.A degrees, B.A. and B.S. degrees, M.B.A.s, and Ph.D.s are now available online from accredited, prestigious institutions, including Duke University, George Washington University, University of Maryland, Columbia University, and Vanderbilt University, and the number of public and private institutions providing distributed degrees is continuing to increase.

One Coin, Two Sides

The College of Liberal Arts and Sciences at Iowa State University honors selected faculty members as master teachers for their ability to teach large classes effectively. To fifteen-year classroom veteran and associate botany professor Jim Colbert, responding effectively to students' questions is a key ingredient to successful teaching. For that reason, Colbert set up an Internet site to collect questions in a non-threatening setting where students could see the questions that other students were asking. The questions themselves inform many of Colbert's class content decisions. He typically opens each lecture by answering the most frequently asked questions.

On the other side of the coin, there are teachers who receive support via the Internet. For decades, teachers have been a primary market for continuing education. The natural benefits of Web-enabled courses apply to teachers as well as other professionals. Real estate, law, medicine, engineering, and dozens of other professions have long required continuing education. Online teacher training is available from the University of Phoenix, Capella University, The Fielding Graduate Institute, Sylvan Learning Systems, and others. E-teaching Institute, a division of eCollege.com, is a professional development site created for educators interested in developing the skills to successfully bring technology into the classroom or teach online. The number of commercial education firms considering marketing courses to educators is growing, including the nation's largest for-profit manager of public schools, Edison Schools.

Somewhere between the classroom-heavy, on-campus approach and the Internet-heavy, online approach is a balanced approach that attempts to retain the best features of both. One such provider is The Fielding Graduate Institute in Santa Barbara, California. Fielding offers accredited masters and doctorate degrees in education, human and organizational development, and clinical psychology. Founded in the early 1970s, The Fielding Graduate Institute is a pioneer and model for distance education. As computer technology evolved, Fielding established its own intranet, FEN (Fielding Electronic Network) which allowed for frequent communications between faculty, students, and administrators. Personal attention is central to its precepts and structure. Fielding is both distributed and tutorial at the same time.

Through years of development and refinement, Fielding maintains a devotion to personalized interaction holding local, regional, and national seminars and conferences throughout the year to promote a sense of true community among students, faculty, and administrators.

Among the many advantages of e-learning is flexibility. Time spent in corporate learning sessions is usually time spent away from regular work responsibilities. Flexible e-learning ignores the clock and the calendar to increase possibilities for integrating work responsibilities and learning opportunities.

In a *Forbes Magazine* special report on e-learning, well known researcher Dr. Brandon Hall claimed, "depending on the complexity of the topic and the individual skill level, some students will learn faster or slower than others will. E-learning allows students to learn at their own pace. The slower student can review course material as often as necessary, redoing exercises or simulations until the information converts to knowledge. An average of fifty percent time savings has been found when comparing time-to-learn in a classroom versus on a computer."

Clearly, online technologies that make information and knowledge more accessible are playing an increasingly larger role in organizational success. This is why organizations are allocating more time for learning at the same time that learning is becoming a more self-directed activity. E-learning courses by and large eliminate the need for employees to travel for educational purposes. Employees can also take advantage of the on-demand nature of most Internet-delivered courses to incorporate learning time into their own schedules, thus reducing the need to leave critical job functions to attend classes.

A fifteen-year study at Stanford University concluded that technology-based learning is of equal or higher quality than conventional classroom training. E-learning will not completely replace classroom instruction, except where it can reduce costs and improve learning. In many cases, e-learning provides a new set of tools to enhance classroom experiences and plug the classroom into the rest of the world. Classroom instruction may always be the best modality for certain types of learning and will continue to be a favorite learning environment for some individuals.

Focused instructional design, interactivity, and student control over the learning process all contribute to Web-centric training having a more lasting effect on the learner, whether technology is integrated with classroom instruction or not. E-learning courses, independent learning, and programmed instruction have been consistently studied since the 1960s in the private sector, public sector, and the military. Results have been consistently positive on alternative learning strategies. It has been unequivocally established that the ease of use, accommodation to learning styles, and improved methods of presentation have an equal or better learning result than classroom-based courses. Because Internet-based courses allow simultaneous training of thousands of employees in multiple regions worldwide with synchronous or asynchronous instruction, e-learning is a gateway to creating a total learning community within an organization, be it local or global.

E-learning empowers students like nothing else has in the past, with responsibility and control for learning shifted into the hands of the learner. The power to conduct research or seek more individualized instruction is another advantage. Competency enhancement and subject mastery don't have to stop when class is over or the course is completed.

Whenever, Wherever, Whatever

E-learning is dynamic and scalable. Resources can be added and expanded with a few clicks on the keyboard and class size can enlarge or shrink at will. Curriculum can be updated at Web-speed and because e-learning can quicken the acquisition and dissemination of knowledge, merging companies can use e-learning solutions to get diversified workforces on the same page in a hurry.

KPMG executive John Green confirmed that KPMG's revenue increases in e-commerce and e-business consulting represent a transformation in benchmarking e-learning's contribution to companies' bottom lines. The company estimated it would have taken three years to train its 22 thousand employees purely through classroom training in its own facility. Using a mix of classroom and e-learning focused around a custom curriculum, KPMG Consulting invested about $3 million to provide 8,000 employees with e-business fundamentals training in twelve weeks. Soon after, the entire workforce completed the program.

Expertise that exists within the learner population can also be added to the body of knowledge. E-learning can exploit curiosity and wonder by individualizing instruction so that a learner's interest is engaged in a manner unique to him/her and the same course content can be taught at various skill levels at various speeds, from remedial to advanced, by the same instructor.

E-Learning: Closing the Gap

E-learning is one of the fastest-growing sectors of the United States economy and the demand to do anything online is growing dramatically. A-lesson.com is a Web-site that helps users find a tutor or private instructor in a variety of fields, including sports, music, and academics. The site also helps both instructors and students find resources in their field of choice. A-lesson.com is also expanding into professional school entrance exams like the LSAT, GRE, MCAT, and GMAT. The site uses a search engine to locate the specialists and other resources instead of putting ads in classifieds or using word-of-mouth.

The National Extension College in England, reports that, "Inquiries from prospective students have quadrupled over the past twelve months." The NEC, with a catalog featuring over 140 offline e-learning courses, is under increasing pressure from students to provide the courses online. IBT Financial, Inc. of Bend, Oregon, is another example of how popular, and potentially powerful, online continuing education has become. As of this writing, IBT, which was founded in 1998, has alliances with thirty-three banking associations, giving it access to 95 percent of the nation's banks with its fifty accredited e-courses.

From e-learning programs at Stanford and the University of Phoenix to computer certification courses at OnlineLearning.net to the online training of health care workers at MedSchool.com, the industry has more than answered any questions about the viability of e-learning. The *"if"* in e-learning is over. It has evolved from the retraining and retaining of IT workers to a universal standard for delivery of training and academic courses. Simply stated, the demand for e-learning hasn't yet begun to taper off.

E-learning: Near or Far

Now that digital communications and interactive media have arrived, the potential of combining electronic media and education has reached critical mass and has permeated education. The debate continues over exactly what to call Internet-centric courses. A widely used term is "e-learning". No one seems to be arguing over the definition of learning, but there is a conversation around the definition of distance. To some, the global reach of the Internet connotes information that reaches persons far removed from the source.

Others think of "e-learning" is an oxymoron. Terms such as "distance learning" and "distributed learning" are common because they focus on the fact that a geographically dispersed group of individuals can be brought together, in real time or at their own pace, at a single online site. The Web networks information everywhere, anytime. The free-market consumer is ultimately in control. Communities of interest and communities of practice are coming together as never before.

E- Learning vs. Distributed Learning

One of the geographic realities of traditional universities and corporate universities alike has been their central locations. The concept of satellite campuses has grown over the years. University of Phoenix has over one hundred local satellite campuses (which is another dimension in the changing accessibility model), now linked to curriculum available over the Internet.

Mergers and acquisitions also contribute to the changes in corporations and their workforces. A corporation with an organizational population spread across all fifty states has an obvious training and information challenge. One acquisition later and, overnight, the workforce can be spread over several *countries*. All of this creates networks of networks.

Examples abound. GeoLearning Inc. of West Des Moines, Iowa, for example, reports that over 30,000 students from sixty-five countries have taken, or are currently registered to take, Internet-delivered courses using the company's online system called Geo Learning Center.

Motivated but heretofore under-served students from rural areas of the United States to the farthest reaches of Uzbekistan will be able to tap into the finest teachers from elite universities. The international dimension of the Internet raises interesting customer service issues. It is one thing to answer questions from United States military personnel stationed oversees, and something else to respond to a request that arrives written entirely in Spanish or Hungarian. It would be beyond the scope of existing tech-support centers to be staffed with individuals who speak every language in the world.

The GlobalLearning Alliance™ is working on portal partnerships that are truly global. The alliance, sponsored by GlobalLearningSystems™, has sixty training locations in fifteen countries providing multi-language programs in various formats to large, global corporations. A showcase for the alliance is VCCN™, the Virtual Classroom Campus Network which leverages a montage of e-learning content through the Internet. Such total e-learning solutions are in continuously greater demand as business and the educational community reach for new ways to answer the question, "how can we learn with no limits?"

Tracking Progress

Individuals progress at different rates. One independent variable is the intensity of the learning experience. In a classroom scenario, learners are expected to move along at a similar rate—with some margin for reasonable variations in absorption. Classroom instruction requires a tandem pace. Faster learners lose opportunities while instructors tutor slower learners, and slower learners are left behind as instructors attempt to find a pace that suits the average learner. This process has served American education for more than a century but it is clearly more targeted to mass, not *individual* learning.

Updating Content

If companies do not have the best people creating the best products, they cannot compete. E-learning provides dynamic, self-directed learning environments that, in turn, improve performance and profitability. Maximizing intellectual capital gives a real competitive edge."

The Growing Popularity of Learning Online

Peter Drucker's *Reinventing the Corporation* was a major bestseller among business readers. Another title for this book could have been *Reinventing Learning*, which has always been Drucker's theme in his classes at Claremont Graduate University in southern California. It comes as no surprise that some readers of this text are reading it over the Internet since it is also available as an e-book online.

Student body demographics are changing and colleges and universities can no longer afford to think of students in the same old ways. Eighteen-to-twenty-somethings are no longer the only students on campus—the virtual campus that is. The increasing opportunities to study are not the only motivation for mid-career adult-learners to crack the books again. It is becoming more and more important for professional men and women to keep up with a rapidly changing world of knowledge either to move up in their careers, to switch careers, or both. It is not only what you know, but how you come to know it that is influential. And how old is the information?

As a testament to the fast-changing world of knowledge, older learners will soon comprise 60 percent of the worldwide student population. 84 percent of four-year colleges are offering e-learning courses in 2002. This is up from 62 percent in 1998. That impressive figure doesn't account for existing e-learning institutions or virtual campuses.

Recalling televised coverage of the John F. Kennedy assassination, the Viet Nam war, the fall of the Berlin Wall, Operation Desert Storm, and now, the terrorist attacks on America, one cannot help wondering how different those learning experiences would have been if television had an interactive capacity. On the Net, chat rooms about worldwide events are springing up everywhere.

Education has become a life-long activity and the Internet is the most efficient means of providing access to this phenomena. The community is the campus and the citizens are the students.

The 2000 budget for continuing education in the United States was $162 billion and $500 billion worldwide. Internet users in other countries are quickly buying up American education and the continuing education budget by no means accounts for the entire online educational market.

Overall, the expectations for worldwide e-learning are impressive. Cisco Systems' CEO John Chambers has been repeatedly quoted for his prediction that, in the not-so-distant future, "e-learning will make e-mail look like a rounding error." Clayton Ajello, president and CEO of LearnWare International Corporation, led his firm in a year-long search for a strategic partner who would provide capital to enable LIC to boost its presence in the healthcare industry.

Ajello found his strategic partner and got his desired funding but, instead of searching for twelve months, as one might expect, Ajello had to bar the door from would-be venture capitalists. "Dot-com" companies may have fallen from popularity among investors, but the growth potential in e-commerce, and especially e-learning, is still remarkable. Security issues have become more critical than ever before and as a result, the e-world will likely become more linked together. Telecommuting can eliminate the stress of rush-hour trips to and from the office and offer alternatives to working in centralized, high-density environments.

Heat On the Street

Arguably, one of the hottest forms of IT training is the Help Desk. Every time someone drops down the Help menu on a computer screen, they are seeking an answer to a technical question. The Help menu at the top of the screen is a non-stop resource for technical training or, at the very least, technical assistance. And so it is with online or telephone tech support. All are hybrids of IT training, no matter what application is being used.

Coffee shops, hospitals, and cable television all operate twenty-four hours a day. Similarly, online support, telephone tech support, and Help menus are there when you need them. E-learning models are also becoming similarly flexible and as more e-courses are offered on the Web, more technical expertise will be required of the learner in order to study. Tech training will take new forms and will find new levels as the telecommunications industry rebounds and booms.

EduCommerce

Just when you thought you had all the angles figured out, along comes notHarvard.com. As the name implies, the company has no affiliation with Harvard University in Cambridge, Massachusetts. The irreverence is intentional and the new trend is innovative—and controversial. NotHarvard.com packages online classes offered by other organizations such as Barnes & Noble University and CodeWarriorU.com by Metrowerks. The catch? The courses are free.

It is the same concept as commercial television (at least the way it used to be). It has been said that television programs merely take up time between commercials. The same can be said for the online courses offered through notHarvard.com. The courses merely put banners and advertisements in front of you. And the advertising is where the rubber meets the road. In a similar fashion to the way cable franchises now make viewers pay to see television commercials, notHarvard.com's clients generate revenue from the free courses.

NotHarvard.com reports that class sizes range from 750 to over 1,000, with some classes as large as 5000. The drop out rate is 5 percent. The courses are free, but the course materials are not. Metrowerks charges $49 to $100 for their software, and textbooks are $15 to $60 each. If you're studying literature at Barnes & Noble University and don't have a copy of the book being discussed, a few clicks of the mouse and the book is on its way to your door—or available for download.

Many "new solutions" companies such as Global Learning Systems, e-Higher Ed, Quisic, Knowledge Planet, Click to Learn, and Smart Face offer material which strives to improve:

- Basic job skills
- Individual and team productivity skills
- Sales performance
- Presentation skills
- Management effectiveness
- Leadership
- Process Improvement
- Experience and knowledge transfer
- Workplace issues
- Customer service
- Communication skills
- Project management
- Call-center performance

The above are central to the new services being offered by the new generation of solutions companies. These are e-learning components that really bring e-learning to life. These companies specialize in blended training a process of effectively integrating e-learning technologies with traditional training methods. The benefits include:

- Decreased learner costs
- Less time away from work
- Increased high-level performance development
- Personalized coaching and mentoring
- Electronic performance support

Pinpoint Accuracy

For workers who have difficulty finding time for workplace learning, or resist it altogether, the more specifically related the learning experience is to their jobs, the more likely employees will want to participate. Courses that are relevant to a worker's departmental or vocational expertise and needs are the most welcome. The closer the course is to the center of the employee's interests, the more likely the worker will learn.

Settling

Anyone who has ever built a new home has experienced "settling." The structure's final resting place is not determined until long after construction is completed and the dwelling is occupied. So it is with the new trends in electronic learning.

The story began with electronic learning technology in its relative infancy. Not so long ago it was little more than classes delivered over telephone lines. Computer bulletin boards attempted to bring teachers together with students. Now, online learning covers a broad range of choices from e-tailers selling custom educational software to companies that create the infrastructure for corporate training courses.

The potential market is huge. In 1999, electronic learning accounted for only $500 million in revenues out of the $96 billion for-profit education market in the United States. Even though the e-learning share of the market will most likely continue to grow, there will be an inevitable shakeout among the top players. Twisting an economic cliché a bit, even though the water in the harbor rises, not all the boats will rise with the tide.

Like the ocean's food chain, big fish will try to swallow smaller fish and some fish, regardless of their size, will fall prey to attacks by other fish who attack either alone or in groups. Investors have grown in sophistication through the rise and fall of the dot-com mania and are better informed, asking tougher questions about profitability. They are also asking for larger stakes in young companies in return for their investments. The *"dot gones"* have cleaned out the market to a great extent and the years ahead should bring a significant rebirth of the telecommunications sector, and especially the e-learning companies. Tramatology, security training, and education in government, healthcare, education, and commerce will boom.

One example is Prosoft Training.com. This young company spent $50 million compiling an enormous amount of valuable content and setting up 45 satellite training centers. What the company didn't do was attract customers. CEO Jerry Baird joined the group, pared down the staff from 300 to around sixty, and focused on marketing the tremendous content that the company had assembled. The firm bestows the title "Certified Internet Webmaster" on its graduates. The certification is now recognized across the country as proof of an individual's Internet skills. IBM, Hewlett-Packard, Intel, DigitalThink, Inc., Arthur Anderson, and Smartforce are now among the many companies doing business with Prosoft.

Brandon Hall said it well by writing: "Like all industries in the New Economy, the e-learning industry is growing at Internet speed and is affected by the same growing pains as other "e" entities in the marketplace. Like other technology industries, the landscape is changing on a daily basis. Over the past few years, technology has changed, improved and reengineered virtually every business process, and now e-learning is reshaping how human resources within our companies are developed."

It's A Wrap

Workforce learning is growing in strategic importance within organizations around the world. Shorter business cycles, faster product roll-outs, accelerated mergers and acquisitions, and increasing competition and knowledge obsolescence mean that revitalizing skills, learning about new products and new lines of business must become ongoing activities. E-learning solutions are now invaluable to deliver fast, flexible, high-quality learning. As the e-market continues to mature, more end-to-end, customized solutions will become available to provide strategic planning services, content, and enhanced communications around the world via distributed e-earning networks.

The best is yet to come.

*Nothing happens
unless it is
first a dream.*

—Carl Sandburg

If I Only Had a Brain
The Fundamentals of Understanding How the Brain Works in Learning

In order to understand human development, one must have a relevant understanding of the learning process. Learning is a function of the relationship between a learner and a learning experience. It is important to think about this as we blend together physical and theoretical learning theories, and the Internet and new media. Each of these concepts is central to understanding how people learn.

Understanding the brain and behavior, and the brain and learning, is important in order to understand the learning process. Part of the process of understanding learning requires understanding the main aspects of the physiology, as well as the psychology, of learning. This includes recognizing the brain as a *learning machine*. Understanding media and learning psychology includes basic knowledge of theories and features of external and internal stimuli, and their implications for learning and behavior. In a sense, to have a true grasp of learning theory one needs to understand learning from the outside in, and the inside out. This chapter deals with the physiology of learning a relatively new, little-known dimension of the total learning paradigm. The next chapter will address theories of learning from the psychological aspect.

This chapter is somewhat technical; its purpose is to underscore the importance of the brain in learning and to add another root to the learning tree explained in this book. To explain, the roots are (1) the importance of K–12 to the future of learning, (2) the dramatic impact of new media and learning technologies, (3) the emergence of the corporate university, (4) the emergence of the CLO, and (5) the nature and theories of learning.

It is important to first be acquainted with the concepts and terminology used in this chapter. Therefore, we have developed the following glossary of terms you will encounter, as well as a diagram of the human brain. Although not intended as an expert review, the following is an overview and examination of the physical and theoretical aspects of learning.

Brief Glossary of Key Concepts and Technical Terms

- The human brain: A three-pound, walnut-shaped organ the approximate size of a small coconut with an astronomical number of interconnections.

- Hemispheres of the brain: The brain is divided into two hemispheres called *cerebral cortex* (commonly known as the conscious and cognitive thinking center).

- The corpus callosum: Tissue separating the halves of the brain.

- The thalamus: directs incoming information to the appropriate part of the brain for further processing.

- Hypothalamus and pituitary glands: adapt the body to the environment by constantly adjusting hormones.

- Hippocampus: Involved in securing long-term memory

- Amygdala: registers and regenerates fear and other emotions.

- The brainstem: carries information from the body into the brain and establishes general levels of alertness and such automatic tasks as breathing, blood pressure, and heartbeat.

- Neurons: the primary building block of the brain, which carry electrical charges and make chemical connections to other neurons.

- Axons: long fibers (extending from the cell body) that transmit messages.

- Dendrites: Short fibers (surrounding the cell body) that receive messages. They grow at different rates during different periods of life and have a relationship to language, mathematical, and musical abilities.

- Synapses: tiny gaps between axons and dendrites (with chemical bridges) that transmit messages. They can wear down with over-stimulation, and can regenerate with rest and reduction in stimuli, including stress.

- Myelin: a sheath that serves as insulation and allows electricity to flow between the axons and dendrites.

Recently, there have been significant new discoveries in understanding the physical nature of the brain. These new discoveries offer a rapidly growing number of insights into the way we learn. Our three-pound brains are like a dense web of interconnecting servers, or synapses that, in many ways, work like a complex web. The brain is an engineering marvel. In a sense, the brain is similar to, and an extension of, the Internet and represents a growing and converging "network of networks."

The vast and seemingly endless connections comprising the World Wide Web put many of us in awe. Yet in comparison, the interconnections of a single brain astronomically exceed the connections of the Internet. It is even more powerful to imagine the physical brain as part of a constellation of wireless and wired server-enabled networks. What a limitless way to think of ourselves.

The typical brain has approximately 100 billion neurons, and each neuron has between one to 10,000 synaptic connections to other neurons. The intricacy and the sheer number of brain connections are majestically extraordinary. We are now only at the first threshold of understanding how our brains work in learning. In the past decade progress in understanding the human brain has been parallel to the progress made in digital technology and communications. For the first time, psychologists and technologists are beginning to think together. The dawn of the twenty-first century is experiencing a biotechnology phenomenon.

Like the Internet, our brains are suffused with a vast number of interdependent and synergistic networks, and all incoming information is processed through those networks. All information already stored in our brains influences how we learn and what we learn.

Glenn Jones, cable industry icon and CEO of Jones Knowledge Group, says that the human brain is the best-organized, most functional three pounds of matter in the known universe. He explains that the brain responds to the Beatles, the Sistine Chapel, automobiles, World War II, Beethoven's Ninth Symphony, Hamlet, Key Lime pie, and matches wits with the increasingly sophisticated, brain-replicating facets of the newest computers.

The brain is both emotional *and* cognitive. Each of these capabilities directly relates to learning, and also to how the Internet and media affect learning. Brain-based learning, using the Internet and new media methods, represents a type of convergence. Those who conceive and design media and Internet-centric learning systems will be wise to study brain physiology and learning psychology so they may begin to build programs using the necessary fundamentals for effective learning products.

Increasingly, the most advanced solutions architects and program designers are factoring brain-based learning theory into their thinking. It is important to learn how to take advantage of the growing body of evidence that neurologists and educational researchers are uncovering about the physical process of learning. As noted earlier, this chapter will focus on those physical aspects and the next chapter will focus on learning theory. These concepts are fundamental in understanding how we learn.

Increasingly, researchers are doing diverse and intricate studies providing more and more useful, valid, and reliable information about the most basic operations of the brain. This new physical research includes studying the normal and abnormal actions of neurons, the synchronized actions of neural networks, and factors that trigger or stimulate neuronal activity. Results of research are reaching a wider population. Applied learning theorists are studying and applying this new knowledge in many innovative ways, including examining the implications of media on brain-centric behavior. Recognizing this trend toward better understanding of the physical brain is an important step in evolving an up-to-date approach to understanding learning. For that reason, let us look at some basic facts about the brain so that we will have a common point of reference.

Each brain is different from the other. As with fingerprints, facial characteristics, and DNA, no two human brains are exactly alike. However, there are numerous universal functions. In all brains, for example, every nerve cell (neuron) serves as a relay station. Neurons receive signals from other nerve cells. Neurons also process the signals and send them on to other nerve cells across tiny gaps called synapses. Chemicals called neurotransmitters cause the signals to flow from one neuron to another. This is an electrochemical process and is the basis of all human behavior and learning. Every time you speak, move, or think, electrical and chemical communications are taking place between tens of thousands of neurons in your brain.

As a nerve cell is stimulated by new experiences and exposure to incoming information from the senses, the nerve cell grows branches called dendrites. Dendrites are the major receptive surfaces of the nerve cell. Imagine a porcupine whose spines are receptors. One nerve cell can receive input from as many as 20,000 other nerve cells. With use, you grow dendrites, or branches. With lack of use, you lose part or all of those branches. The old adage, "Use it or lose it", is becoming a fundamental principal in new understanding of brain function. This discovery has become central to new knowledge about how we learn language, music and mathematics and will be discussed in greater detail later. Thinking of the brain as a muscle that grows through use and diminishes with lack of use is creating growing interest and agreement in visualizing the brain as a learning machine.

Plasticity is the ability to change the structure and chemistry of the brain in response to the environment. The concept of plasticity is important when thinking about one's brain development.

Current research indicates that dendrite production is greater at certain periods during our lives than at others. Studies on language learning show that dendrite production is greatest in young children. That is one reason significant language learning takes place in young children. Early exercise of language, music, and mathematical brain function can have a major effect on one's later life facility with language, music, and mathematics.

Some have called the 1990s the *"Decade of the Brain."* This is because scientists were able to start using new technologies such as Magnetic Resonance Imaging (MRI), Functional MRI (FMRI), and Positron Emission Topography (PET) scans. Technologies such as these help researchers understand how human brains process cognition, memory, emotion, attention, patterning, and context. All of this information is leading us to greater understanding of the learner and the learning experience.

Renate Numella Caine and Geoffrey Caine, co-authors of *Unleashing the Power of Perceptual Change: The Potential of Brain-Based Teaching*, validate the idea that our brains are whole and interconnected. "Even though there are a multitude of specific modules with specific functions, thought, emotion, physical health, the nature of our interactions with others, even the time and environment in which we learn, are not separated in the brain. They are not dealt with one response at a time."

While many brain centers function independently, the brain is essentially in touch with all of its parts simultaneously. This is quite incredible when you think of it. There are literally hundreds of topics that brain-based learning research is examining. The remainder of this article will explore a cross-section of major subjects that relate directly to learning, the relationship of the learner to the learning experience, and which are influenced by the physical nature of the brain.

Attention

In commerce, attention is treated as a commodity. The phrase, "pay attention" is used so commonly that we hardly realize the importance of its meaning. For purposes of this description, we will explore the physical nature of attention and also address the psychological nature of attention. The thalamus, located near the center of the brain, plays an especially important role in attention. The thalamus is the "relay center" between our sense organs and the brain's cortex. This process separates the important information within our short-term memory systems, apparently sorting and ignoring the less important information. This seems to create the visual awareness we experience that catches our "attention"."

Eric Jensen, author of *Teaching With the Brain in Mind*, reports that our bodies have high-low cycles of energy that relate to attention. Each of these cycles is about 90 to 110 minutes in length. This relates directly to attention. When students are at the top portions of those cycles, they're more attentive. At the bottom of the cycle, energy drops along with the level of attention. Jensen suggests that educators and trainers recognize and "learn to ride with the cycles," which will increase effectiveness. At the very least, realizing that attention is likely to be periodic and cyclical offers a strategy when designing media-based programs. Cycling a key concept related to attention, and attention is central to learning.

Motivation

Motivation stems from some form of anxiety. Anxiety is stimulated by fear. Renate Caine talks about the different types of motivators and what happens in our brains depending on the source of motivation. "When we encounter high stress in learning, there is a psycho-physiological response to the threat, accompanied by a feeling of helplessness or fatigue. This type of response blocks or keeps people from using their higher order, more complex thinking, and creativity." So, excessive complexity or fear can have a blocking effect on learning. People who frequently block may develop a *learned helplessness syndrome*, which will be discussed later.

During high-stress situations, information physically takes the primary pathway through the thalamus and amygdala and then moves into the cerebellum. Memorization of isolated facts can be accomplished under high-stress conditions, but higher order and creative thinking may be lost. We tend to respond with either a primitive mode of behavior or with early, programmed behavior. Simply put, emotions generally dominate cognitive processes. In a sense, we are emotionally, or amygdala, driven. That is why the joke that you spent your child's college money on a Porsche, probably has a grain of truth. Feelings of safety, comfort, and relaxation are enhancements to learning.

The amygdala functions in relation to all emotion. It is the sensor for stress, and most significantly, "fear." Recent studies at Duke University even suggest that how we perceive color is a survival reflex. In addition, there is new research on the effects of color on perception. If a person were consciously aware of the color of the neckties worn by each of the candidates during the 2000 presidential election, one could identify the persona each candidate was attempting to project to voters.

In situations that may involve stress, but in which we have a sense of control or choice, the physiology changes. Without stress, the primary path of data is not directly through the amygdala, but through other paths of the cerebral cortex that are involved in higher-order functioning. Thus, we avoid a "knee jerk response" that is driven by emotions.

Therefore, learning situations that are low stress favor reflection and analytic thinking. Caine states that, "The thalamus, hippocampus, and cortex (where stored memories are housed and higher-level thinking takes place) are all involved. With this system, you can translate factual elements and make connections. Also, you can make inferences based on other things you know. That higher-order thinking includes synthesizing information and integrating it to come up with new ideas." Knowledge is the lowest level of understanding application is a higher order, synthesis yet higher, and combining synthesis and application to create new knowledge is the highest level of human functioning. Therefore, the highest level of learning is using what has been learned to create new knowledge.

Context and Patterns

"Without context, emotions, or patterns, information is disconnected and meaningless, so we experience incoherence. Within people, there exists an innate and natural propensity to try to form some kind of meaningful pattern out of learning. *Meaning* is helpful to our survival and our brains are always trying to make sense out of incoming information streams.

Jensen says that, "While the brain is a consummate pattern maker, intellectual maturity and experience often enrich the process." Interestingly, PET scans indicate that a novice chess player burns more glucose (i.e. has to work harder) while using the step-by-step sequential left side of the brain than does a more experienced player. A master chess player uses less glucose and engages larger patterns from the right side of the brain." The left side of the brain is generally thought of as the cognitive or factual side, and the right side the affective or theoretical side. It may be that the right side of the brain is crucial to the ability to be creative and to project solutions.

Research done on recent memory processes indicates that recent memory also involves pattern-making abilities. Several studies have asked participants to read a long list of words. When a participant is asked to remember certain words on the list, an interesting results often occur. For example, let us say the list has twenty-five words strung together, including cake, cookie, sugar, train, candy, tree, car, and dog. If asked whether the word sweet is on the list, for example, most participants say yes because the words cake, cookies, and sugar evoke thoughts of sweet. Interestingly, the area of the brain that registered the other words on the list lights up on an MRI. This means that in trying to make sense out of a word, the brain also makes connections and picks up inferences. That clearly illustrates significant scope in of brain-processing mechanisms. The brain makes connections and generalizations even though, in many cases, the generalizations may be wrong.

What this means is that when detail is not sufficient, a conclusion is still drawn, though not always correctly. The brain doesn't have values; it's an information organ. It isn't an arbiter of values or of right and wrong. What we do have is a system that puts related events together in hierarchies and categories and what determines one's response to this information is context and culture. So while we are dealing with the internal brain function here, it is obvious that understanding the external influences is critical.

Geoffrey Caine states: "The brain mind naturally organizes information into categories. We can generically call that 'patterning.' These patterns always involve interpreting information in context. There's a great deal of research to show that we learn from peripheral perception as well as from focused attention. When people are forming patterns, a lot of the information that brings the pattern together is peripheral or contextual information." Understanding results from a combination of physiology, heredity, and environment.

Emotion

We described the emotional center and the amygdala earlier. Now, let's expand our understanding. The amygdala is a small, almond-shaped area within the brain, located near the hypo-campus, and hypo-thalmus, and is believed by many neurologists to be a center for human emotions. According to Jensen, this tiny amygdala has twelve to fifteen distinct emotive regions and it often exerts a tremendous influence on the cortex. "Information flows both ways between the amygdala and the cortex, but many specific areas are involved in subtle emotions," Jensen claimed in his work. The amygdala is thought to be an emotional center and the cerebral cortex a cognitive center.

"Making daily decisions based on emotions is not the exception…it is the rule," says professor Antonio Damasio, a neurologist at the University of Iowa, in his book *Descartes's Error: Emotion, Reason, and the Human Brain.* "While extremes of emotion are usually harmful to our best thinking, a middle ground makes sense. Appropriate emotions speed up decision making enormously."

As noted earlier, brain research shows that emotions and thought are deeply interconnected. In *Molecules of Emotion,* psychologist Candace Pert writes that on the surface of every cell in the body are receptors that respond to molecules such as various peptides and neurotransmitters. Scientists used to think that those neurotransmitters were found only in neurons in the brain, but it turns out they are in every part of the body. When we have a thought, many of the peptides and neurotransmitters interact with cells throughout the body, and those interactions trigger what we call "the experience of emotions." That is why we feel the emotional response throughout our total body, and explains why the emotional response is so powerful.

"Good learning engages feelings. Rather than viewing feelings as an add-on, therefore, emotions are part of the learning experience. Emotions surface when we search for meaning and predict future learning because our goals, beliefs, biases, and expectancies are right brained, affective and emotional. Emotions drive the threesome of attention, meaning, and memory," says Caine. Emotions reinforce and amplify learning. Positive emotions can be a tremendous asset in facilitating learning.

According to Professor Daniel Schacter of Harvard University, author of *Searching for Memory,* there are two possible explanations for the way emotionally charged events are imbedded in our memories. One is that stress hormones and chemical messengers, or neurotransmitters, are released at such times, which "tag" the event with special significance and give it prominence in the memory pathways. The other explanation for what are commonly known as "flashbulb memories" is that even though they don't need to be rehearsed or reiterated, they usually are. "People tend to discuss and go over the things in their lives that are important to them, and that strengthens the memory," says Schacter. Repetition is central to establishing long-term memory.

Dopamine and the Workplace

People with increased amounts of chemical dopamine in their brains show improved episodic memory, working memory, verbal functioning, and flexibility in thinking, creative problem solving, decision-making, and social interactions. Caine points out that the climate of the workplace is critical to the kind of product you're going to get. If we feel supported in that environment, the physiological effect is a slight increase in dopamine, a neurotransmitter, which releases the correct amount of acetycholine (another neurotransmitter that stimulates the hippocampus).

Memory, Recall, and the Brain

One of the most spectacular uses of recently improved imaging technologies such as CAT scans, MRIs, and FMRIs is to show the brain at work—thereby helping researchers understand memory, recall, and how we manage information and information overload. "Memory is the ability to repeat and re-conceptualize a performance. Physically in the nervous system, memory is manifest through dynamic populations of neuronal groups. Unlike computer-based memory, brain-based memory is inexact. It is also capable of great degrees of generalization. Memory would be useless if it couldn't in some way take into account the temporal succession of events—of sensory events as well as patterns of movement," says Edelman. At the moment, this phenomenon is central to the debate about whether computers can ever simulate the human brain. It is a great debate—and we really don't know how far we can go.

Rita Carter, who wrote *Mapping the Mind,* says that new neural connections are made with every incoming sensation and old ones disappear as memories fade. So understanding both short-term and long-term memory is important when studying learning. "Each fleeting impression is recorded for a while in some new configuration, but if it's not laid down in memory, and preferably repeated, the pattern degenerates and the impression disappears like the hollow in a cushion after you stand up." Patterns that linger may in turn connect with, and spark-off, activity in other groups—forming associations (memories) or combining to create new concepts.

Many of us have heard the phrase, "etched in my brain," referring to memories that seem indelibly imprinted in our memories. We now know that there is some physiological fact attached to that saying. The function of memory rests upon these facts. There is a biochemical process called Long-term Potentiation (LTP). Simply put, brain synapses fire and re-fire again and again, but never in exactly the same order. LTP is the process that accelerates a synergy between specific neurons after a *significant* connection is made. "Significant" could be almost any unique experience, such as watching a horse race for the first time or seeing a professional boxer fight for the first time or hearing a composition by Mick Jagger or Mozart for the first time. The experience causes a unique pattern of neurons to fire sequentially, and those sequential firings cause connectivity. The sequential connections are sensitive to one another and can be re-triggered again and again, though not in a completely identical order. This re-firing is thought to leave a permanent, physical etching of the original sensation. These long-term physical memory traces are called "engrams" and engrams are perhaps one of the reasons we are able to become addicted.(Kotulak, 1997)

Our memories recall the pleasure we associate with a specific experience. If it is a pleasurable experience our minds want to repeat it. One of the reasons habituation may be so very hard to break is that the more times we experience a particular situation, the more difficult it is to "overwrite" the engramatic patterning or "etching" in our brains. Often it is harder to un-learn than to learn, and for that reason, it is very important to have both good fundamental instruction when learning something new, as well as a pleasant experience. The human desire for pleasure is very basic. A good experience is something we do not choose to forget easily. The interpretation of *pleasure* may be completely subjective to each individual. These thoughts form a part of my theory on positive addiction.

Feedback Loops

Brain activity creates a constantly changing internal environment, which the brain then reacts to as well. That creates a feedback loop that ensures constant change. The loop-back process, sometimes referred to as "neural Darwinism," ensures that patterns that produce thoughts, and thus behavior, and that help one thrive, are permanently embedded, while those that are determined to be useless fade.

According to Carter, it seems that incoming information is split into several parallel paths within the brain, each of which is given a slightly different treatment depending on the route it takes. Information that is of particular interest to one side of the brain will activate that side more strongly than the other. Using a brain scan, you can see that happen. The side that's in charge of a particular task will light up while the matching area on the other side will glow less brightly.

Geoffrey Caine reminds us that when we can connect rote memory with ordinary experience, we understand, make sense of things, and remember more easily. To transfer information effectively, we need to see the relevance of what we are learning. This leads to connected concepts such as positive psychology and positive addiction.

Richard Restak, a neurobiologist, writes in *The Brain*: "Learning is not primarily dependent on a reward. In fact, rats—as well as humans—will consistently seek new experiences and behaviors with no perceivable reward or impetus. Experimental rats respond positively to simple novelty. Studies confirm that the mere pursuit of information can be valuable by itself and that humans are just as happy to seek novelty," sometimes translated through curiosity.

Human beings tend to be both curious and motivated. According to research by Robert Aitken at Vancouver Community College in British Columbia, staying motivated may be a conscious human choice. This is the difference between a human and many lower animals.

Human beings are naturally motivated by curiosity and stimulated by novelty. So, if one is emotionally engaged, learning can take place. The emotional quotient can be as minor as novelty, or as significant as fear.

Motivation may be examined from several different points of view. We can pursue the same distinction between intrinsic and extrinsic motivation. Intrinsic motivation has to do with what we want, need, and desire. It is hereditary and physiological. Abraham Maslow established his hierarchy of hereditary needs. Which is grounded in human values and feelings. Someone else trying to make us want to do something often stimulates extrinsic motivation. In terms of learning and creativity, we know there's a positive correlation between creativity and intrinsic motivation. When we are organizing information in our minds, the way we form patterns is deeply motivated by what we're interested in.

From the perspective of learning and a healthy brain, the most exciting discovery is that education should, and can, continue for a lifetime. With enrichment, we grow dendrites; with impoverishment, we lose them at any age. Work-life and lifelong learning are important key concepts for healthy living.

In summary, this chapter has provided an overview of the physical aspects of the brain as it relates to learning, and has presented a general understanding for those interested in learning, learning systems, the Internet, and new media. The purpose of the chapter is to give you a framework for understanding. The development of learning experiences, wherein we are trying to create an understanding between a learner and the learning experience requires that the developer understand the intrinsic and extrinsic factors involved when using media tools for communication and stimulation. It is important that a Chief Learning Officer have some depth in understanding the technical aspects of learning, and a Chief Executive Officer should at least be familiar with terminology.

The brain functions like a muscle. New research on the physical brain is teaching us a great deal. What we know now is, if you exercise your brain it will work better and longer.

In Chapter 7 we will explore extrinsic theories of the new learning psychologies and we will continue to address these in the context of performance improvement, the Internet, and new media. Relating the psychology of learning, including the study of the brain as a learning muscle, provides fundamentals for teachers, media professionals, and anyone else us interested in learning as it expands capacity for understanding.

Learning Theories

E-learning is a tool to enhance human performance.
Learning theory is a fascinating and extensive topic to
examine. Since this book addresses the Internet, media
and learning, we have approached the broad topic of e-
learning theory in the context of telecommunications and
media. Learning how to learn represents a primary concept
that is fundamental to the goals of e-learning.

There are certain principles that are fundamental
to all learning. To fully understand the potential of
e-learning strategies, one must grasp the implications
of learning styles, specific intelligence, and theories of
human development and systems. Individual learning
styles, literacies, and specific and multiple intelligence
are essential factors to be understood and applied when
producing and designing e-learning experiences. Without
understanding these theories, it will not be possible to
appropriately strategize the use of pictures, graphics, and
sound fostering the learning experience. There are new
literacies to be understood when dealing with media. These
subjects are the basis for this chapter on learning theory.

Learning Styles

Two fundamental questions with respect to individual learning: How do people learn? and Why do people learn? The ways in which individuals learn are tied to heredity and environment. Heredity and environment are also reflected in one's personality. The physical aspects of learning are discussed in chapter 6. This chapter examines theoretical aspects of learning. There are countless variations in human personalities. We will examine a few of the general categories of personality type as examples. Combinations of traits comprise different personalities. Different individuals learn in different ways. This is a basic principle to understand and apply when designing learning systems. Choice and options are fundamental in accommodating diverse learning styles. Most learning software has had a focus on the "how." Here, we will be focusing on the "why."

E-learning, with significant audio-visual and interactive power, is one of the best tools we have to help personalize and individualize learning experiences. Individuality determines how one takes in information and translates information into knowledge. How much a learner retains and applies from a learning experience is, to a significant extent, directly related to how well the learning experience matches the individual's learning style and how many senses are involved in reinforcing the experience. One size does not fit all. In addition, personality and learning styles are determined in the early years, 0-7 years of age. Therefore, forcing an individual's learning style to fit a rigid, pre-determined format is not the best way to facilitate learning. The traditional classroom is a group-management method, not necessarily the best teaching/learning method. One-to-one instruction is the goal of all learning strategies.

Motivation is a key to learning. As a motivational enhancement it is important to make sure workforce learners understand the organizational reasons for learning. Anyone in charge of a learning initiative should be conscious of the behavioral outcomes desired. Learners are often subjected to poorly designed content that can produce outcomes disappointingly similar to outcomes that result from under-motivated learners. The learning system and strategies can handicap the learning experience.

To Each His/Her Own

If you are planning to create access to a course across your organization, be sensitive to the fact that salespeople invariably learn differently than computer wizards, and computer wizards invariably learn differently than clerical staff, or machinists, or engineers, etc. Numerous factors, including personality and genetics, influence why individuals choose their particular career paths. The same genetic and environmental influences that differentiate one personality from another serve to differentiate learning styles. If you stop to reflect on learning experiences throughout your life, you will probably notice some patterns of your own.

Even an activity as common as distributing straight-forward announcements around an organization should be done with an eye toward tailoring the information to various personalities and learning styles to make the communication effective. This is fundamental to the concept of the learning organization.

The Broad Categories

Four main learning components comprise a learning system. Two broad learning categories are different types of *perceiving* and different types of *processing*. In perceiving, there are two subcategories: *concrete perception* and *abstract perception*. Processing also has two subcategories: *active processing* and *reflective processing*. The implications to e-learning represented by these categories vary widely. The objective here is that you are conscious that there are different ways of perceiving and processing.

Concrete perceivers learn best by doing. Concrete perceivers pay attention to their senses and feelings. They are eager to put knowledge into action. Learning programs that emphasize hands-on experience and practice lend themselves to the concrete perceiver's natural tendencies. E-learning can supply a variety of simulations to keep a concrete perceiver's mind and hands busy. The greater the activity level, the more the concrete perceiver absorbs, retains, and applies.

Opposite of the concrete perceivers are the *abstract* perceivers. Most forms of e-learning, especially e-learning delivered over the Internet, favor abstract perceivers. The abstract perceiver prefers to think about items. The abstract perceivers are the ones who wore out the encyclopedias in the library as children. They like to watch, study, and analyze before making up their minds.

Abstract or concrete mechanics of e-learning should be considered when producing all interactive formats including CD, DVD, intranets, or expanding access throughout the World Wide Web.

Processing

The concrete perceiver is most likely an *active processor.* Quick to act, eager, and impatient to apply new knowledge. The active processor may toss aside an instruction manual without reading it, preferring to "shoot from the hip." There is some inherent liability in this approach as the active processor feels the need to "do" in order to grasp new knowledge. As previously mentioned, there are many grades of these learning styles, however, generally speaking, for the active processor, e-learning programs that offer lengthy explanations and long examples are not effective unless they involve *doing.* Active processors are likely to say, "Show me once and then get out of my way" or "If you tell me, I'll forget. If you show me, I may remember. If you let me do it, I will 'get it.'"

In contrast, the reflective processor might say, "Let me see that again," or "Now that I've seen the demonstration, I'd like to think about it." Even after a hands-on learning experience, the reflective processor may need to reflect on what took place in order to make sense out of it.

The Best of Both Abstract and Concrete Processing

Thomas Edison was widely regarded for his genius and innovation. Edison had interns in his laboratories. Those young people represented the top of their classes at various universities. Edison frequently gave his interns problems to solve. One day he asked them to determine the weight of the water required to fill a light bulb. The small group split up and worked on the problem all day. Late in the afternoon, they each presented Edison with their answers. Without exception, each intern had applied this formula or that formula and performed complex calculations to arrive at a figure.

After all the interns had reported in, they anxiously waited for Edison to reveal the correct answer. To their surprise, the inventor took a light bulb, put it on a scale, and weighed it. Then he removed the base, filled the bulb with water, replaced the base, and weighed it again. By subtracting the weight of the empty bulb from the weight of the full bulb, he determined the weight of the water.

Edison probably never cared about how much water it took to fill a light bulb. The point that he so effectively made with his interns is similar to what we are saying about e-learning. There are times to be linear and times to be non-linear, times to experiment and times to use imagination. Sometimes it is best to have a concrete perceiver in charge, other times an abstract perceiver will work best. Sometimes the simplest, most obvious solution is bets and sometimes it is not.

Intelligence

Human intelligence is most commonly defined as the capacity to learn and understand. Learning happens in different ways for different people. Learning and understanding results in intelligence, but until very recently, intelligence has been determined by how it is assessed, rather than how it is gained. Yet, research by Professor Jim McGraw at the University of California, Irvine, indicates that intelligence quotients (I.Q.) can be raised up to twenty points through continuous exercising of key mental activities. Conversely, without use, I.Q. can diminish to the same degree.

Cognitive I.Q.s are calculated based on instruments that measure how well individuals collect, organize, and interpret data. Accurate data or relevant interpretation is not a factor. The ability to test well with collecting, organizing, and analyzing data has a direct effect on high cognitive intelligence scores. Theoretically, it was thought that emotions and other senses do not come into play in traditional intelligence testing. We now know that is not necessarily the case. Anxiety can diminish processing capability and capacity and individuals with hyperactive disorder (HD), attention deficit disorder (ADD), or a combination of both (AD/HD), test differently than individuals without those conditions.

Contemporary thinking on the subject of intelligence focuses on the notion that the very concept of intelligence has traditionally been too limited for appropriate, universal application. The concept of *emotional* intelligence emerged to help explain that people are smart in different ways. Before emotional intelligence, the concept of *multiple* intelligences was added to the emerging cognitive/ emotional intelligence dichotomy. As we explore emotional and multiple intelligence more deeply, we should be mindful that individuals learn differently because of sensory styles and also because of specific *intelligences*. The work of Howard Gardner has been central to establishing the validity of multiple intelligences.

In the same way that awareness of multiple learning styles gives us ways to teach people more effectively, the concept of *multiple intelligences* helps provide a roadmap for positioning individuals within learning situations or organizations where they will be most effective and also gives guidance with respect to e-learning software. The concept of multiple intelligences gives us a clearer picture of how people learn. Professor Howard Gardner at Harvard University has developed the theory of multiple intelligences. The eight intelligences defined by Gardener are presented in the following chart.

Intelligence	Description
Verbal-Linguistic	This is our ability to use words and language and has tremendous impact on our ability to use digital electronics as a teaching and learning tool. Verbal-linguistic intelligence is one of the primary criteria used in traditional learning and intelligence assessment.
Logical-Mathematical	This is our capacity for inductive and deductive thinking and reasoning. It also describes how we use numbers and recognize abstract patterns. Logical-mathematical intelligence is also emphasized in traditional schooling and intelligence assessments.
Visual-Spatial	This refers to how we visualize objects and dimensions in space, as well as how we create internal images and pictures. Sometimes individuals with highly developed visual-spatial intelligence are described as abstract thinkers.
Body-Kinesthetic	This is the body's language that controls physical motion. Tensing up in reaction of a potentially conflict situation is a kinesthetic response. The whole range of body language falls into this category.
Musical-Rhythmic	This is our ability to recognize tonal patterns and sounds. This category also includes sensitivity to rhythm and beats.
Interpersonal	Interpersonal intelligence is highly developed among those to whom person-to-person communications and relationships come easily. Persons who experience difficulty interacting with others have a diminished capacity when it comes to interpersonal intelligence.

Intelligence	
Intrapersonal	self-reflection and awareness of the inner, spiritual state of being. Some people who have a knack for one-to-one interaction are not so comfortable with looking inward.
Environmental	Environmental intelligence relates elements, including climate, atmosphere and objects, surrounding an experience, and their effect upon that experience.

Multiple intelligences, or ways that individuals develop, also govern styles of learning and communication throughout life. The eight primary intelligences identified by Gardner describe how we perceive and understand the world and they also represent the manner in which we resolve conflicts. These theories are all part of the complex human learning puzzle. All learners favor some forms of intelligence over others. Developing specific intelligences leads to new aspects of literacies.

Grasping these concepts is fundamental strategic understanding for modern organizational leaders. Organizations cannot survive for long without enlightened leaders. In the rapidly changing environments within which public and private sector organizations operate, organizations that fall behind have little hope of catching up again.

> *"Parents often look with contempt upon video games played by children. Yet, video games teach children something that many failed businesses should have learned: 'standing still will kill you.'"*

(Robertson Stevenson Study, 1998)

New technologies that are changing the way we communicate and learn. Commenting on learning and new media, Gardener notes that new technologies make materials vivid, easy to access, and fun to play with. New technologies address humans' multiple ways of knowing.

Columnist Ruth Palombo Weiss states, "Gardner believes that as people become more comfortable with electronic media, the media will become indistinguishable from earlier, more familiar forms such as books or graphics." Media literacy is emerging as an accepted phenomenon. Using the work of Gardener and others, new theories of multiple literacies are now emerging.

Interestingly, the late author, educator, and scientist Isaac Asimov (1920–1992), once told me that as far as he was concerned, there are probably 1,000 or more specific intelligences. What is important to realize is that each separate intelligence may be developed. There are multiple intelligences, therefore, multiple options and literacies support the long-articulated principal of multiple learning styles.

I.Q. vs. E.Q.

Let us examine cognitive and emotional intelligences. Dr. Reuven Bar-On, the author of the EQ-i and the person who coined the term "emotional intelligence" (EQ), said that it has been scientifically demonstrated to his satisfaction that emotional intelligence is of equal importance in predicting success in the workplace as a cognitive intelligence. Bar-On calls the truly intelligent person someone who is not only *cogtelligent* (cognitively intelligent) but also *emtelligent* (emotionally intelligent).

Emotional intelligence can be described as awareness, sensitivity, coping, and management skills that enable us to achieve our goals. Allowing emotional issues to impede personal success is not considered emotionally intelligent. Cognitively intelligent people are often referred to as *smart* and an emotionally intelligent people are referred to as *stable.* Certainly it is possible to be both smart *and* stable, but every person's composition is going to differ, by a little or a lot.

Today's solutions architects are keenly aware that it is important to have stable people, as well as smart people, running organizations. From an organizational and systems design standpoint, a cognitively intelligent person will contribute most to an organization when dealing primarily with data collection and analysis. A person with high emotional intelligence is energized by human contact. When describing a person with emotional intelligence, the terms "intelligent" and mature are often used interchangeably.

According to Steve Hein of the EQ Institute in Clearwater, Florida, recognition of multiple intelligences helps productivity by developing intrinsic motivation that increases employee commitment, cooperation, and cohesion. Lost time spent on conflicts, turf-battles, defensiveness, and insecurity is reduced.

Authors Cary Cherniss and Mitchel Adler take a more encompassing view of EQ. *"The increasingly global nature of business, the growing reliance on technical innovation, and rapid downsizing have created an organizational need for employees who are capable of interacting smartly."* Emotional intelligence is an important aspect of learning because emotions override cognitive processes in the learning experience.

Learning Theory

We have now looked at the theories of learning styles, multiple intelligences, and multiple literacies. Now let us explore high concept analysis. Examining the dozens of learning theories individually and relating them to an equal number of learning strategies is not practical at this point. We are going to present several of these concepts. However, those who are specifically charged with the responsibility of designing courses and curriculum need to study these topics in great depth. Provided is an overview for awareness, challenging you to more effectively champion the cause of e-learning in your organization, and to be flexible and sensitive to intercultural differences, dissonance, available options, alternatives, and preferences.

Sensory psychology, i.e., synesthetics, examines the experience created by combining one sense with another. In addition, semiotics, which is the study of the identification and use of symbols including icons for program navigation, and semantics of language will be addressed in chapter eight.

Pictures, graphics, sound, and their convergence, are the

ingredients of the psychologies of e-learning, and the new educational and media psychologies.

Let us now examine three basic areas of learning theory: behaviorism, cognitivism, and constructivism to help us expand our thinking. Behaviorism deals with observable changes in behavior and generally assumes that behavior can be improved. When the issue is improvement or mere modification, behaviorism focuses on a new behavioral pattern that is practiced until it becomes automatic. Cognitivism examines the thought processes behind the behavior. Thoughts cannot be observed until they are translated into an action. Observable behavior is the best indicator as to what is happening inside an individual's mind. Constructivism deals with reality, specifically the premise that we all develop our own perspective of the world through direct experience and/or information that we receive. However, that construction is manifested in behavior.

Behaviorism and E-learning

A good illustration of behaviorism comes from the field of drama. An audience cannot read what is on an actor's mind, but can only observe what s/he does. The audience members cannot see murder in the mind of an actor, but they can see the acts, such as changes in facial expressions leading to the action of murder. At that point, the behavior makes obvious what is going on in the actor's mind. The action illustrates the thought.

To many, computers are technical/mechanical boxes within which all kinds of things take place that we don't see until the computer displays something visually, emits a sound, or causes something to happen like turning on a light, firing a reentry rocket, or dispensing money. Behaviorists are similar in that they think of the mind like a box where thought processes take place, and the proof of those thoughts is in the behavior. Behaviorism is simply examining the outcomes of the learning experience.

There is a behavioral phenomenon called "spontaneous recovery," which, in the context of e-learning means that learned information that slips from the learner's consciousness from lack of application can be resurrected with re-exposure to the learning experience or key elements of the learning experience through which the behavior was modified to begin with. Spontaneous recovery is the reason that practice is important. Repetition has the result of embedding behavior so that it can be recovered.

By its nature, e-learning can be replicated in part or in whole by the learner at will. Instructional designers can make sure that the learners keep encountering fragments of the new knowledge by *salting* them through new materials, long after the primary learning exercises are over. This capability to keep the learning alive through continuous communication gives Web-delivered e-learning a distinct advantage over traditional learning formats through facilitating repetition. The term for behavior disappearing after removal of the stimuli is termed "extinction." Extinction simply means eliminated from memory. Related factors that enable repetition strengthen desired behavior.

Summarizing Behavior, Cognition, and Construction

Behavior, cognition, and construction support the exercise of intelligence. Organizational learning is an evolving strategy in many organizations. As an organizational leader it is your responsibility to understand that e-learning solutions are more than classroom courses uploaded to the Web. Today's solutions are diverse. The nature of both classroom and non-classroom media-centric learning is changing dramatically, and the concept of the "learning organization" is central to organizational function.

If you want to explore the subject of learning theory further, you can visit such sites as the Theory into Practice (TIP) database at www.gwu.edu/~tip/index.html. TIP contains descriptions of fifty theories relevant to human learning and instruction, and again, offer an opportunity for you to learn through "Casting the 'Net Over Global Learning."

Ten Key Concepts of Human Learning and Motivation

To summarize important aspects of this discussion about learning and new media, I have synthesized key concepts important to understanding learning theory.

Freud said that anxiety is the stimulus for all motivation. Fear is the underlying, precipitating factor in anxiety. Anxiety is the trigger mechanism for motivation. Fear and anxiety are both emotionally related. All current research agrees with Freud to the extent that emotion dominates logic. Emotions influence all behaviors. If one looks at the factors related to human motivation and learning and accepts the premise that emotions influence behavior, then you have identified one of the key factors that serves as an enabler in causing learning to take place. The point is that emotions influence all behaviors.

Other factors related to motivation and human learning are:

1. Individuals are influenced by their immediate environment.

2. Individuals are influenced by their past experiences.

3. Individuals are influenced by their perceptions, regardless of the accuracy of those perceptions.

4. Statistical significance and truth are not the same. Learning must be measured by more than just statistics. You may be *statistically accurate* and *actually wrong*.

5. Quantitative research on human learning and motivation is not necessarily accurately predictive. It is well known that college grades are not universally predictive in terms of career success. Part of the reason is that multiple-choice inquiry is only partially revealing because different people select the same answers for different reasons. Therefore, superficial questioning provides only indicative, not accurately predictive, information.

6. Individuals are more receptive to messages if they are consistent with that person's emotional state. This means that readiness is one of the significant factors in human learning.

7. It is easier to learn correctly the first time than to relearn. Unlearning and relearning requires a shift in belief or behavior and such shifts always encounter resistance. Learning requires energy. Learning is driven, to some extent, by how much energy one must expend to achieve a desired state.

8. Defenses play a critical role in some learning. Therefore, it is an increasingly growing factor in our emerging multi-ethnic social structure.

9. When we recognize that all of the Fortune 500 companies are global, the importance of their context becomes clearer. All of the Fortune 500 transcend geography and culture.

10. Multiple intelligences are synergistic with multiple literacies and multiple learning styles.

Continuing our study of theories of e-global learning, we may begin with the sage words of scholar, scientist, and visionary Isaac Asimov,

> *"Creationists make it sound as though a 'theory' is something you dreamt up after being drunk all night."*

The theories in the list that follows are not specific to media psychology. However, understanding them is essential to your professional development, the development of media software, and a true understanding of the Internet, new media, and human learning and motivation. Therefore, the following theories are presented as a basis for further study on your own. Please email me at bjluskin@cs.com to discuss any of these theories or concepts further and I will attempt to respond.

Emerging theories related and important to learning, software, media, and Internet psychologies include theories of:

Trying

Success

Failure

Learned Helplessness

Intelligence

Mastery

Psycho-visualization

Believability

Hypnotic Induction

Color

Sound

Graphics

Situational Cognition

Positive Addiction

Attention

It is my plan to elaborate these and other theories in the next volume in this series.

This chapter has launched your overview of learning with respect to new media, the Internet and human development. The new learning psychologies that are related to media are emerging and they are being refined. Clearly, it is not possible to go into elaborate detail in a single chapter. A more in-depth elaboration of those issues will be covered in the next book being written in the "Casting the 'Net Over Global Learning" series. Having learned how to learn we can share and learn together and continue casting the 'Net over global learning.

The Psychologies of Producing Media

Preparation for writing this chapter began with my keynote address to the SALT (Society for Applied Learning Technologies) conference in Florida in 1996 (subsequently resulting in an article entitled Media Out of Your Mind, first published in THE Journal in 1998) and a second keynote presentation at SALT in 2001. I have been developing the concepts presented in this chapter for many years. I continue to expand my research of these concepts, including new developments in the application of Sensory and Media Psychology, to the production of media software and e-learning systems. This work has now led to courses and programs in the psychologies of media, online learning, and new learning theory. It has led to a graduate program in media psychology at The Fielding Graduate Institute.

In this book special focus is also given to the implications for the emerging new corporate university as an education and training mechanism, and the positions of CLO and Solutions Architect, as examples of increasing expertise emerging in e-Media. Since my original presentation, the

Nobody motivates today's workers. If it doesn't come from within, is doesn't come. Fun helps remove barriers and boosts motivation

—Herman Cain, CEO, Godfather's Pizza

American Psychological Association has adopted Media Psychology as an approved sub-specialty in psychology, several professional journals dedicated to the subject have been launched, and university programs have been established in recognition of the need to understand the use of sensory media and media psychology as *intellectual technology* necessary to the construction of good programming using e-media and communications technologies.

"Marquee psychology" is a term used to describe the use of prominent products and celebrities to create increased stature and appeal of products to buyers and audiences. Motion pictures such as; *Star Wars, E.T.,* or *Harry Potter,* CD-ROMs such as *Compton's Encyclopedia, Myst,* or *Dragons Lair;* and product containers such as Campbell's Soup and Coca Cola are examples where marquee psychology has been central to driving the success of a product.

This chapter examines the underlying psychology upon which programs, courses and services are developed. It describes the nature and scope of the psychology of producing media. The future quality of education software—whether on campus, on the Internet, or television—will be driven by a new look and feel in the twenty-first century. Now, with breakthroughs in wireless and portable handheld devices such as the Compaq Ipac, and developments such as Web-enabled DVD, whole new approaches to the use of media in education and training are emerging. Companies such as Click Vision, Vidyah, K-12, Quisic, BrainX, etc., are leading the way.

Producing media software is a communications craft. The successful producer must combine the knack of thinking visually, drawing upon a myriad of techniques taken from communications arts including film, photography, writing, painting and more, so that s/he can manipulate media elements and use them to produce compelling programs.

People use a variety of terms including human factors, ergonomics, cognitive engineering, user psychology, sensory psychology, or media psychology to describe various aspects of producing media. Each of these terms has its own inferences and nuance of meaning. As new concepts emerge, so does a new vocabulary.

When examining the psychology of producing media, one immediately discovers many complexities and dimensions. Examples of sub-specialties and new psychologies are: (1) the psychology of persuasion; (2) the psychology of editing; (3) the psychologies of sound, color, attention, cognition, control, games, and (4) the psychology of learning styles. Each of these topics is a subject unto itself.

It is not possible to examine all of the facets of the psychology of producing media in one chapter. However, we can look at examples and analysis to help show the nature, scope, and technique of production psychology and subsequently build on that information.

We know more than we understand. Great progress will come through understanding what we know and using it.

—Bernie Luskin

The Psychology of Editing and the Importance of "The Point of View"

All editors are essentially created equal in terms of technical resources. The technology of editing is quite advanced. The X-factor in non-linear editing is the "human factor." With music, for example, music theory and the practice of music principles provide the foundation. The human factor, that is called *talent*, brings a wonderful, almost charmed, distinctiveness to the application.

Non-linear editing represents an art form. This is especially true when storytelling. We all perceive and experience events. When we go from place to place, such as driving to the market, we experience certain perception edits. While driving, we notice scenery and cars as they pass. The car's engine and radio provide context, continuity, and language. Music may influence mood. When we open the door, we step out into a new environment. When we enter a building by passing through doors, or climb a stairway or look up at a light, we change points of view.

Whether editing a linear story or interactive scenario, combinations of edits show and tell the story with a perspective. Storytellers need a vision to communicate or an idea to share. There are always multiple editing choices employed in recognition and perception. Perceptions are created with varying degrees of sensitivity. Without "accurate empathy," which requires "seeing through the eyes of the beholder," the perceptions are inherently flawed. The psychology of editing represents one of the many emerging, sophisticated specialties in our changing media world. Editing in a way that stimulates emotion, creates understanding, and rivets attention requires the highest level of editing skill.

The Psychology of Emotions

As a second example, let us examine further the psychology of emotions discussed on in the previous chapter. Sensory psychology, or *synesthetics*, represents the study of the experiences resulting from a uniting of the senses. Adding one sense to another facilitates an experience of higher intensity. This concept is central to stimulation strategy in media. Think of how the impact of a silent film can be enhanced with the appropriate sounds.

Synesthetics is the response occurring when one sense is added to another. It is perhaps the research that is most critical to the development of media psychology's emotional dimension. In the new media, the user's total environment is based on multi-sensory responses to various audio-visual elements.

Synesthetics, coupled with television or computer interaction, creates sensory rivalry and may create positive or negative experiences or reactions to information, ideas or presentations. Each stimulus may create positive or negative experiences or reactions, conflicts of cues, or sensory rivalry. The result, in any case, is emotion from a union of senses stimulated by the multimedia experience. For example, seeing a boat rocked by waves may activate a sense of imbalance in an observer to the extent that it causes seasickness. Viewing a painting of an Arctic scene filled with frost and snow may evoke the sensation of icy cold, producing goose bumps. Hearing an explosion or gunshot may trigger the illusion of being attacked. Most of us have looked at pictures of appetizing food and, in turn, felt sensations of taste, smell, and hunger. Each of these examples represents a potential behavior or psycho-visual result engendered by a multimedia interaction.

To create the behaviors or responses we seek, we must use the psychology of editing described earlier, plus the psychologies of color, sound, movement, situational cognition, and storytelling when creating scenarios.

The Psychology of Language

Semantics represents the incisive use of language. Managing language is fundamental to communication and central to our ability to understand. One simple example may be seen when examining the use of the word "quit." "Quit" is a pejorative term of frustration that means "to give up." "Quit" also is a software programming term that is used by programmers when writing code. Unfortunately, it has found its way into the interface of many programs. The subliminal response to the word "quit" is negative when it is used in educational or consumer programs.

Better choices would be "end" or "stop" or "pause" because those words imply appropriate meaning without the implications of failure that the word "quit" conveys. Words and their use, articulation, alliteration, intonation, and patterns, are central to media communications.

The Psychology of Symbols

Semiotics is the study of signs and symbols in human communication. Semiotics plays a very important role in media because the manipulation of visual symbols facilitates the human-machine interface. Symbols should help understanding, communication, and the creation of relationships. Icons enable navigation and control over media pathways and the clear, creative, and careful use of symbols gives rise to iconography as a highly developed semiotic skill.

The graphic interface, through which information is made accessible onscreen, is the principal point of contact between the machine and people. Graphic interface design, iconography, and navigation strategies are basic programming architecture and emerging insight to the most effective use of symbols. They represent fundamental skill requirements for those who use media in communication. Microsoft, Netscape, Yahoo, and other media producers continually search to find symbols and methods that are intuitive, friendly, representational, and easy to use.

These few examples illustrate the range and scope of production-related media psychology. The various aspects of media psychology are manifested in techniques, based on principles of psychology, that give us practical parameters and techniques for producing better, more compelling programs.

Production Techniques

Let us look at some principles of media psychology. The following twenty-two production techniques are essential to making better programs and exemplify some of the concepts described earlier.

1. Uncluttered backgrounds are better for image clarity and comprehension. A straightforward presentation is generally best.

2. Narration should be conversational with significant voice modulation. Dull, boring, monotonal documentary-style narration of the past is not sufficiently energizing. Jack Nicholson, Charlton Heston, Meryl Streep, and Danny Glover are some of the narrators with whom I have worked who absolutely understand what they are saying and speak with energy and modulation. Monotone or clinical, emotionless narration is one of the perpetuated myths of documentary production. Sound sets the mood and affects what one sees. An audience sees with its ears as well as its eyes.

3. Fading to black is normally not effective. Fading to blue or another default color, or dissolving from one image directly to another image makes a presentation look more seamless. These techniques remove jarring transitions from image to image and improve the relationship between visuals. Remember that black is the color of a "crash" in computer software.

4. A program should never take control away from the user. The user should be able to interrupt the programming, and skip to another activity or choice at any time. Taking control away from the user breaks concentration and implies the program knows more than the person using it. Freezing interactivity and forcing the user to wait for a "message" or a play function before being able to continue or exit makes the user feel like a hostage. Users should always have the choice to bypass messages.

5. Too many buttons or icons are confusing. Keep the number to a minimum and make the symbols simple, internationally generic, and *very clear.*

6. Avoid the tendency to over-design and under-explain control features.

7. A good "how to" is critical to almost every program. Interactive content is invisible. Many educators and professionals in the industry agree that a very simple, linear "how to" is best—even in an interactive program.

8. Music heightens emotion and increases the enthusiasm and energy of participation. Research shows that appropriate music increases the viewer's perception of pictures, sustains mood, and provides pace.

9. Some activity on the screen is preferable at all times. Activity attracts and helps hold attention. Dead screens lose attention in a very short time.

10. Fonts must be large, clear, and legible. Avoid tightly packing in large amounts of small text. Many users are quickly frustrated by having to squint at small font. Make it easy to see.

11. Contrasting colors are clearer from eight to ten feet away. This will be relevant as TV-PC software comes into vogue and the user is sitting on a couch, not at a desk.

12. Dead ends in navigation create confusion and frustration. All interactive programs should always have a reasonable number of branches.

13. Text messages must be short and very carefully edited. The wordsmith is clearly an important media craftsman.

14. Underscoring text with voice narration gives text much greater impact.

15. Too much content in a program is as bad as too little. Encyclopedias may be designed so that one will never see the material, but with most products, there must be a sense of completion and accomplishment to create satisfaction for the user.

16. The look and feel, structure, content, art direction, and functionality are each programming elements that should be evaluated separately and together.

17. Scripts should be written and spoken using proper language, avoiding both slang and overuse of contractions. Regional accents tend to narrow audience identification with the narrator, and subsequently, the material being presented.

18. *Transparency* is the key to the link between the mind and emotions of the user and the content of a program. All intervening functionality needs to be as self-evident as possible to remove any guesswork that interferes with access. Keep it simple. If the user needs to get from A to C, let him get there without having to go through B—if that is his or her preference. Try not to manufacture interference. Make the interface as transparent as possible.

19. The "you attitude" is basic to content, script, and user-centered activity. Use of the word "you" places the focus upon the receiver of the information and is a basic of good communication. "You" attracts the interest of the person whom you are targeting and engenders a measurable emotional reaction.

20. Control bars in interactive media should be just that, interactive and selectable, unless there is a compelling reason to freeze them.

21. Highlighting text with background color makes fonts easier to read.

22. Every program should have a linear play mode of some sort. The "how to" may serve a dual purpose in certain circumstances. Without a linear play feature, a clear grasp of the content may elude many users. Sometimes users many choose to be led. They should not have to struggle too hard to discover or understand the "strategy" of the navigation design. To paraphrase Marshall McLuhan, "The message is the message" and there are times when a linear explanation serves the user best.

PC- TV Convergence

The difference between the PC and the TV is rapidly disappearing. Networks of PC and TV communications will be common in our new century. The "screen-ager, Webhead" generation looking for PC cinema, and the cyber-patrollers speaking "Webonics" and dreaming virtual dreams are now alive and well. This evolution into the cyber-generation has significant implications for all society in the new millennium and particularly for our industry. This paragraph, and this book, may seem as though it carries substantial jargon. This is, however, the language of media now. The future of media is "screen deep," and rife with new words and meanings. As noted earlier, Web-enabled DVD will facilitate the new communications strategies. The new Sony Game player, Play Station II, Xbox, and most of the new players are computers with DVD drives that also connect to the Web. They are Web-enabled to combine data from the Web with computer data, overcoming bandwidth limitations.

During the 1980s the spread of the PC and the growth of productivity software was exponential. Laser and digital advances marked the 1990s as the "decade of the gadget." Cheaper, smaller, faster gadgets and appliances proliferated. However, the quality of much of the programming still has a long way to go. In this first decade of the new century we will experience a blizzard of new media programming and production techniques. As a result, psychology is becoming more and more significant and media psychology is providing the basic principles underpinning all quality productions. A new media literacy is emerging as understanding the specifics of media and behavior becomes more important than ever before.

Over 100 years ago, the psychology of media shifted significantly from still photographs to moving pictures. Until 1914, all cinematic cameras were static, locked in one stationary position. Legendary director D. W. Griffith, had the insight to move the camera while filming his masterpiece, *Birth of a Nation,* thereby forever changing the nature of filmmaking and allowing audience members to have their own "point of view" for the first time. Griffith, using his genius to experiment with angles, lighting, make-up, and editing cuts, stimulated the earliest thoughts about the psychology of the various aspects of storytelling through movie making.

The science of motion pictures advanced through silent films to "talkies" and by the 1950s, the first widespread use of color-processed negatives came to the screen. The 1980s brought better sound and the 1990s gave us computerized morphing techniques, transactions, and interactive technology. The early twenty-first century is bringing recognition that there is a new media psychology to be understood and applied throughout all of education, training, and telecommunications.

The nature of TV is moving from passive toward the first degrees of interactivity. The PC is expanding from its role exclusively within the framework of productivity toward a position within mainstream entertainment. In the 1980's the PC was seen as a work technology and the TV as an entertainment technology. Stereotyped perceptions still dominate, but as interactive television, satellites, and wireless communications improve and change, perceptions will also change. "Interactive television," via the PC or the TV, will be the medium of tomorrow.

Leadership Makes the Difference

Now is the time to foster greater understanding of what it takes to make the programs and services people want. The motion picture industry provides a good model for understanding production in many media for two main reasons. First, the industry has the most production experience (over one hundred years—with experimentation and innovation by the most creative people of each generation). Second, the movie industry, by virtue of a century of worldwide distribution, is responsible for instilling a level of expectation in the general public for the way productions should look. The industry has created a demand for American cinematic-quality production values. The areas of photography, art direction, sound editing, special effects, musical scores, lighting, screenwriting and adaptation, directing, editing, and all other stages of pre-production and post-production provide a media model with a century of success upon which to draw. The global public has come to expect from every screen a high level of production quality, no matter that the screen is television, PC, 70mm Imax, or handheld Compaq Ipac.

Achieving the potential of media in our future means unlocking its power through understanding. At this stage, leadership may become the most important single factor in advancing the social and industry understanding of media and the new telecommunications world. Dwight D. Eisenhower used to demonstrate the art of leadership with a simple piece of string. He would put the string on the table and say, "Pull it, and it will follow you anywhere. Push it, and it will go nowhere at all." Producers should lead by example.

In the context of leadership, media communications can create richer, more elaborate relationships to enhance commerce, healthcare, politics, education, and entertainment. Practitioners must understand the "why" as well as the "how" of media production. It is no longer enough to produce by rote or formula. One must understand the psychology of media production to make good programs: People are driven by their emotions when they are correcting a deficiency, engaging in personal development, or simply having fun.

Future Developments

Technology will not be the defining feature of successful media—new media and technology will create an essentially *new environment*. The ten factors listed below serve as examples of key developments that will be central to this environment:

- A new grasp of sensory media
- Broadcast is being replaced by access and power and control is moving into the hands of the user
- Technology and high quality sensory programming (messages) will reshape many markets
- Real-time networked communities of people with shared interests will heighten communication between people
- Communication is getting more personal, rather than less personal with the proliferation of personal preference channels among a thousand other reasons that are part of the shrinking world
- The market trend toward self-service will grow significantly
- Competition will increase because of variety and diversity
- Personalized brands will become much more common
- Wireless digital communication will link everyone, everywhere, even in the most remote locations
- Programming of all types will be produced in new ways

The discipline of the psychology of producing media will become part of many university programs dealing with all forms of media. It will also become critical when researching ways to improve the media and in making technologies more effective and user friendly. It will extend to all commercial fields, and to the development of media for physically, psychologically, and mentally challenged populations. The psychology of media production is now fundamental to successful programming for education, training, commerce, entertainment, religion, healthcare, and politics. Understanding the principles that comprise the basis for the psychology of production is imperative for all professionals in the burgeoning new programming and services industry of the next century. E-solutions architects will comprise a new breed of media and Internet developers. They will understand the effects and affects of media upon behavior, combining systems theory, theories of human development, technical media, sensory and media psychology in ways that bring forth a new wave of software and programming for this new century.

Producing media is a communications task and media communications, both sophisticated and straight forward (such as e-mail), are central to the future in casting the 'Net over global learning.

K–12, The Learning Continuum, Work, and the 'Net

The 2001 Web Commission of the Unites States Congress strongly urges greater acknowledgment of the importance of the learning continuum from kindergarten throughout our entire lives. The commission particularly underlines the importance of early learning as fundamental to individual personal development and later life accomplishments. In short, the key to competitive success and advantage for both individuals and companies in the twenty-first century is *early* learning, learning, learning. We now have research information supporting this position; this chapter enumerates some of that research.

More than ever, learning, education, and training are determining the quality of our lives. Those who do not engage in continuous learning will find themselves living in a world apart. Personal and professional corporate development are now a millennium imperative. Education and training as a marketable commodity are the coin of the realm in the emerging telecommunications and biotechnology economy. Early learning is a key to achieving in this new reality. This

Education and training, as a commodity, will become the coin of the realm in the emerging telecommunication and biotechnologies economy. Personal and professional development is a millennium imperative, and early learning is a key to unlock future workforce competence.

—Bernie Luskin

chapter examines the case for early learning as a necessity for future competitive success.

Webster's dictionary defines learning as, "to gain knowledge or understanding of, or skill in, by study, instruction, or experience."i Learning includes the relationship between a learner and a learning experience and planning is both a significant learning activity and an extremely effective learning strategy in itself. In a sense, the result of all planning is learning. Planning is an effective teaching/learning strategy.

Pre-natal researchers tell us that learning is something human beings start doing before birth. Experience and biotechnology report that we never lose our ability to learn, provided we continually use our learning faculties. Some of us might lose our desire to learn, but learning is living and living, by definition, is learning.

There are many ways to express the concepts of the importance of both early and continuous learning. Biotechnology has validated genetic inheritance of skills and abilities, and the importance of triggering these skills and abilities early in life. Current thinking likens the brain to a muscle that becomes stronger and more effective with use. Lack of use can cause intellectual atrophy. Exercising the muscle increases its capacity.

In a world shaped by an increasingly knowledge-based economy, there is a ravenous, growing appetite for education in both developed and developing nations. Governments, corporations, and individuals are all asserting that education is the path to self-determination and prosperity, and more and more, they are willing to invest in education. Multi-national companies are increasingly recognizing that investing in workforce education is imperative. For the individual, it is a path to a better life. For a company, it provides the competitive advantage.

Results of Early Learning Stay with the Learner

Over 65 percent of American children aged three to five are enrolled in public or private pre-school programs.

Half of the 11 million children served through the federal government's Title I Higher Education programs are in pre-kindergarten to grade six.

Research data now concludes that what a child learns at three years of age definitely affects how he or she will perform in third grade (eight years of age) and later. This is a fundamental reason why children, their teachers, and parents must have access to research-based early learning programs that deliver prerequisite language and early literacy skills. Early learning is a key to later literacy.

The results of early learning stays with the learner throughout life. Years of research now validate that early childhood literacy is more closely tied to an individual's ability to succeed as a functionally literate adult than was previously realized. There is documented correlation between elementary and secondary scholastic performance and economic vitality on a global scale. This high concept perception clearly links early education and the future global economy. Growing confirmation of these facts is leading to significant changes in education. Education is now central to the political agenda of both the Republican and Democratic Parties.

Corporate university expert Jeanne Meister talks about monumental and unprecedented changes taking place in the American education marketplace. Meister argues that one tremendous paradigm shift now taking place is a move from "a government-run monopoly with little accountability, to a market-driven system that competes on price and quality." The business community recognizes that it is suffering more than ever before from the early learning inadequacies and their residual effects manifested by the limited educational proficiencies of young people graduating from high school. What is interesting here is the articulated link between early learning, education and workforce training.

The urban kindergarten to twelfth grade (K–12) educational dilemma represents a growing crisis today. A total of 31 percent of our children don't graduate from high school on time, despite relaxed academic standards and graduation requirements. Of those children who start high school, 10 percent drop out of high school before graduation.

American students score below most students from other developed countries in the areas of math and science. This is happening in despite spending more than ten percent of America's gross domestic product, on education. The U.S. domestic education spend is now second only to health-care spending. With this much money spent, why are good results so hard to achieve?

The K–12 e-Remedy

The K–12 educational market and the adult education markets are separate and will likely stay that way. However, the lack of basic workforce education and skills plaguing employers will not be resolved in the long term unless the K–12 problem is attended to now. This is why an examination of K–12 is important. Let us look at some of the many K–12 initiatives underway.

The Peninsula School District of Gig Harbor, Washington, developed the Anywhere, Anytime Learning Program in association with Microsoft and Toshiba. This pioneering work started when district officials, teachers, parents, and students realized that if the future of educational computing was to be harnessed, they must harness the power of the Internet. The Peninsula School District team worked with Stream Technology Group of Greensboro, North Carolina, to develop a system that would assist teachers and students to find helpful information on the Web in a timely manner. They developed the concept of aggregating the best resources on the Web for use by anyone in K–12 education and the product that emerged is the Copernicus Education Gateway (which may be explored more thoroughly at www.edgate.com).

Teachers in any state may log onto the Curriculum Matrix at Copernicus anytime to find lesson plans, Web-based resources, and performance assessments geared to the standards of the state in which s/he teaches. Local school districts can augment lesson plans available on Copernicus and learn from the experiences of other districts.

Teachers can have individual locations on the Copernicus

site where they can post homework assignments and other information. Parents can have information posted by teachers automatically forwarded to their home or office e-mail address. Information resources available on Copernicus include:

- *USA Today*
- The International Center for Leadership in Education
- *Encyclopedia Britannica*
- Griffin Publishing for the United States Olympic Committee
- EdWorld
- Pearson Publishing
- Flying Rhinoceros
- The Smithsonian Institution
- Voyager Expanded Learning
- The White House
- NASA
- J. Paul Getty Foundation
- National Endowment for the Arts
- Department of Labor
- United States Department of Education

Copernicus also hosts the Partnership for Family Involvement in Education Website for the United States Department of Education. This is important information to know if you are concerned with how the United States will stay competitive in world markets in the years ahead. Our young men and women need to bring value to their employers by entering the workforce with highly developed computer and software skills and the ability to navigate the Internet to find information resources quickly and efficiently.

Dr. Mark A. Mitrovich, former superintendent of the Peninsula School District in Washington State, summed it up, "Today, *speed, connectivity, and the growth of intangible value* are replacing the old education cornerstones of time, access, location, and control." Online learning solutions such as Copernicus are changing the profile of K–12 education in a way that more closely resembles the changing profile of business and industry around the

Professional organizations need to stay in constant communication with their customers and team members.	Copernicus returns time to educators and allows them to stay in constant communication with students and their parents.
Professional organizations need their team members to be savvy on the Internet as well as accountable for their online activities related to work.	Copernicus provides students directed-but-open access to Internet resource and encourages accountability.
Professional organizations benefit from maximum interaction with their customers. Customer online access is the spine of e-business.	Copernicus lets parents stay involved in all aspects of their children's education.

world.

Jeanne Meister connects the life-long nature of learning and the emerging demand for education in the workplace. "Education no longer stops when workers graduate from traditional schools. In the old economy, one's life was divided into the period when one went to school and the period after one graduated and worked. Now workers must expect to build their knowledge base throughout their lives. Work and learning are overlapping in industries as diverse as computer software, health care, utilities, telecommunications, and even training and development."

Degrees and certificates represent ongoing milestones. Each degree means a new beginning; each certificate an acknowledged specialization. In addition, as certain knowledge and skills become antiquated, this knowledge must be revitalized. When knowledge becomes stale and irrelevant, it needs to be rejuvenated. This is the nature of the modern learning continuum.

The Skills Gap

Many people think the skills gap that we read so much about is merely the distance between the number of open information technology (IT) and other workforce positions and the number of qualified individuals to fill them. The U.S. information technology gap, for example, is expected to exceed 1 million workers by 2005. Who can say how large the gap might become before supply catches up with demand?

According to Bill Cullifer, executive director of the National Association of Webmasters, the more exotic the IT skills needed, the harder it is for employers to fill positions. The greatest demand is for those skilled in the "hot" technologies such as Web development.

The term "skills gap" is also used to describe the widening distance between the information capacity of digital technology and the information capacity of the human brain. Since the advent of the modern computer around 1945, the information capacity of microprocessors has increased sharply. Unfortunately, the same cannot be said of the human brain. Studies indicate that the growth of the human brain (volume in cubic centimeters) has remained essentially flat for the last 100,000 years. However, research on intelligence now validates that specific intelligence as well as IQ may be increased through effort. This is a significant realization. Work at the University of California at Irvine reports that an individual's IQ may vary by as much as 20 points (in either direction) based on education and *motivation*.

Moore's Law, formulated by Intel co-founder Gordon Moore, states that circuit density (the number of transistors per square inch on a computer chip) has doubled every eighteen months since the technology was invented. The smaller and more tightly packed the transistors become, the faster they can process data. You could say that men and women in the workplace are at constant risk of being overpowered by their computers. This means the issue of workplace competency in the era of computers is more complicated than just keeping up with the number of computers that have appeared in the workplace over the past couple of decades. Those who use them must stay up with changes taking place just to stay even.

The rapidly increasing power and capabilities of the technology diminished the idea of total mastery of every facet of digital technology and underline the nature of emerging specializations. Intel has announced that it will build transistors with elements as narrow as eight angstroms, or three atoms. IBM has plans in the works to make chips ten times faster than current models. Pentium chips contain 42 million transistors and run at 1.5GHz. The new chips will contain 400 million transistors and run at 10GHz. Getting a handle on rapidly progressing technology requires the use of the technology itself as part of the solution. That means dealing with issues of technical literacy at very early ages and, again, links early learning and future workforce needs. Soon we will have disposable paper cell phones and computers and they will be inexpensive, fast, and portable.

The Need for New Literacies

All organizations now suffer, directly or indirectly, from the erosion of traditional literacy in the workforce. Additionally, there is a changing and expanding definition of literacy now emerging that will be discussed in more detail later on, called "new media literacies."

The shortage of qualified high-tech workers has become so severe that nearly 150 Silicon Valley employers banded together to form an organization called Workforce Silicon Valley. This collaborative project brings teachers into the workplace to gain a better understanding of the work for which they are preparing their students. The teachers work with company officials to identify the types of skills that prospective employees will need to become future valuable staff members. The teachers then work in teams to design courses in everything from robotics to business writing.

This course-designing program is a model now being copied across the United States. Visiting industries yields students who are better acclimated to the nature of the working world for which they are bound and makes the transition from school to corporate life easier.

Professional organizations, both public and private, must now invest in elementary, secondary, and post-secondary education to better prepare their future labor pool. The lack of workforce skills is an acute situation and companies cannot wait for colleges, universities, and business schools to churn out IT-qualified candidates. Without a comprehensive long-term approach, needed progress won't be made. The IT gap is a new workforce problem set in a new time. Recognizing that we have this problem and examining ways to resolve it for our future success is a clear perception of the early learning link.

In technology-based industries, the primary reason that academic preparation is no longer completely sufficient, as in past days of the fixed MBA curriculum, is the dramatically changing nature of digital technology. All aspects of IT are constantly changing. The only way to keep even the most highly skilled employees current is to make continuous learning part of an organization's culture. More and more companies are doing just that because they realize that quality corporate learning programs can reduce the pressure to recruit individuals with just the right combination of skills. Finding an exact fit to fill job vacancies will be much less common than in the past.

A Moving Target

The Digital Workforce: Building InfoTech Skills at the Speed of Innovation…just about says it all. United States Department of Commerce analysts put the number of IT jobs created from 1996 to 2000 at more than 1.5 million. As the demand for technically skilled workers continues to grow, efforts need to be made to interest young people in pursuing technical careers as early as possible. But younger workers raised on digital technology are not maturing fast enough, or in sufficient numbers, to meet industry demand. This is one reason for so much immigration of technology employees from other countries into the United States.

The Department of Commerce has expressed concern with this situation because of the economic jeopardy a technically unprepared workforce will eventually cause. The demand for computer scientists, computer engineers, and systems analysts is expected to more than double by 2010. The growth rate for all other occupations is expected to grow by only 14 percent over the same period. Even those who do not specialize in IT careers need to be increasingly technology-savvy just to function effectively in a work environment that becomes more digital by day.

New media literacies are necessary.

The pressure to bring more IT skills into the workplace is well documented. The unemployment rate for IT workers, before the events of September 11, 2001, were less than half of that for the rest of the workforce and, even following the challenge of terrorist attacks, the IT workforce continues to grow at more than five times the rate of the general work population. With traffic on the Internet still growing exponentially, e-commerce will continue to need more digitally literate men and women. The new security needs resulting from the New York City and Washington, D.C. tragedies have brought new opportunities in the field of communications technology and a new boom in telecommunications is on the horizon. The High-Tech High in Los Angeles, led by Roberta Weintraub (mentioned earlier), indicates this new direction.

There is a surprising development taking place within the federal government, the largest single employer in the United States. With digital literacy on the rise among existing middle-management level employees, the number of employees responsible for strictly clerical tasks has been unexpectedly cut by more than half since 1990. This means that middle-management level executives are using computers on their desks to write their own letters and manage information that was once paper-and-ink intensive and handled by large numbers of assistants.

The composition of the government workforce is clearly changing, just as it is in the private sector. Bolstered by IT skills, clerical workers have begun moving up within the structure of their organizations and new jobs and positions are being accompanied by increased compensation and responsibilities. Simply put, acquiring new and expanded IT knowledge and skill increases one's primacy in the workplace.

The Commerce Department's Office of Technology Policy (CDOTP) helped to define the important distinction between training and education. In describing the "pervasive and fast-paced growth of information technology" in the United States economy, the CDOTP sees the solution as more than training more persons to perform IT functions. Instead, we need to undertake the more challenging role of preparing them for the "ever-changing nuances of technical innovation." The pervasive "just in time" mantra now coexists with the concept of education with "headroom to grow."

This translates into a broader definition of education. Except for trade-specific schools, students emerging into the workforce will need to know specific job-related skills but they will also need to know *how* to learn. To prepare students to become productive employees they must *learn how to learn* as a first step in the concept of *Earning Through Learning*™. This concept is a step forward in "inventing the future of education."

Training vs. Education: Examining the Definition

The terms "training" and "education" are often used interchangeably. We smudge the line that distinguishes one from the other, largely because the terms now overlap in definition and context. In the training industry, however, definitions have been specific. Let's examine distinctions between training and education.

A dog or a dolphin can be *trained* to repeat behaviors on command. So, too, can a human being. When we say that a worker is well trained, what we're really saying is that s/he adequately performs the tasks that have been taught, promptly, efficiently, reliably, etc. A highly trained person may select from a variety of responses to a situation, providing that all of the responses have been properly *loaded* into the individual's memory. We would not say that the same individual is *educated* to perform a certain task in a certain way. Education and learning imply a capacity, and even an expectation, of reflection. We would not expect or even want an assembly line worker who installs windshields to reflect on the cosmic wisdom of installing a windshield every time an automobile approaches him or her on the line. When a product arrives in front of an assembly line worker and s/he observes a defect, the procedure to alert a supervisor is a trained behavior.

Picture two workers sitting side by side at computer

terminals. One is strictly entering data as trained to do. The person on the next computer is composing a letter to a client. Both individuals have been trained to use the computer. Formatting the basic letter is a learned behavior that merely calls for replication of established procedures. But once the letter writer goes beyond the software's formatting protocol and begins to compose a unique message, education overshadows training. The letter writer now makes decisions on the best way to use language to convey a thought or series of thoughts to someone else.

To compose a message that shares information in order to elicit a desired response from the recipient, the writer must reflect on the intent and tone of the message and consider the recipient's range of understanding and response. Rather than replicate a learned behavior, the writer begins making numerous, instant, yet complex, choices. Vocabulary, phrasing, grammar, and syntax all flow from parts of the brain expanded by education.

Even though training and education can be and are often used interchangeably, we define "training" as a process of developing a specific behavior or series of behaviors through instruction and practice. Education is the process of developing the abilities of the mind. "Training" refers to teaching and/or sharpening desired skills while education imparts knowledge and allows for growth. Training may start and stop as needed. In the best of all possible worlds, and workplaces, education never stops. Terms such as "just in time" are applied in workforce training. Training with "headroom to grow" implies education.

At the time author Peter Senge called for continuous learning in his bestseller, *The Fifth Discipline,* many executives nodded in agreement. Most, however, did little to change the role, and priority, of learning in their organizations. As we proceed deeper into the knowledge-based economy, learning is no longer optional for individuals or companies. Basically, training teaches the student how to do something and education teaches the learner how to learn. Anthropologists attribute evolutional progress to our ability to learn and to use one tool to make another tool.

Janice R. Lachance, director of the Federal Office of

Personnel Management, summed it up succinctly by pointing out that one of the most valuable attributes an employee can possess is the "capacity to learn new skills." The benefit of education vs. training includes an atmosphere and attitude regarding continuous learning. Progress in information technology knowledge is moving at the speed of innovation. Innovation requires continuous learning. The knowledge metaphor says that information is the lowest level of knowledge. This is followed by application of knowledge and, subsequently, synthesis that give one the ability to use synthesized knowledge to create new knowledge.

Strong Backs and Strong Brains

Not so very long ago, the majority of workers in the United States worked with their backs, not their brains. This is endemic to Henry Ford's assembly line in that men and women on assembly lines were little more than interchangeable parts of a mechanistic operation. In the twentieth century, blue collar workers were the majority and white collar workers were minority. The balance has now changed, both on the assembly line and in the front office. The highly sophisticated computer-controlled robotic and diagnostic equipment used to manufacture automobiles and other products requires skilled and knowledgeable workers. As office equipment becomes increasingly digital, enhanced skills and training are required.

Technology has helped shift the balance of power and the advent of the personal computer, the Internet, and the electronic delivery of information and dynamic new media are transforming the world from a manufacturing, physical work-based economy to an electronic, knowledge-based economy. As the bar of sophistication continues to rise in the workplace, education is being elevated on the corporate priority list as never before. Education has always been important, but now it is becoming a critical *resource* in the never-ending struggle for success.

The four-year degree represents a protocol of personal and professional life and now reflects tradition. The concept of a four-year, undergraduate degree has changed tremendously since World War II. Prior to the late 1940s, college campuses were, for the most part, the domains of wealthier, more affluent members of society. In those days there were relatively few management jobs in the upper tiers of the professional pyramid as compared to the larger number of labor positions available toward the bottom. Over time, several developments and trends arose to challenge the status quo.

The traditional military model itself represents a sword that cuts both ways. On one hand, the hierarchical structure of the military was the organizational model for business. The officer corps was an elite, educated group, just like the business executives with keys to the executive washroom. The much larger number of foot soldiers parallelled the ranks of laborers on the factory floor. This bureaucratic model served business and government well during the period of manufacturing dominance.

Then along came the GI Bill. Following the Second World War, one of the many veterans' benefits was college tuition. College campuses were no longer predominantly domains of the upper classes. The sons and daughters (mostly male veterans at that point) of working class parents enrolled in colleges and universities and began earning degrees. The rapidly growing post-war economy was hungry for management personnel. Over time, the hierarchical management structure in business, borrowed from the military model, slowly gave way to a somewhat flatter organizational structure as more and more individuals became qualified for management positions.

This democratization in itself didn't drive a stake into the heart of bureaucracy. Evolving technology and the growth of knowledge that accompanied it caused the shift in priorities between muscle and mental dexterity. The movement to flex labor muscle through unionization peaked in the mid 1950s. Since then the most highly populated and politically powerful collective bargaining units in America have become government workers unions, only a fraction of them being factory-type laborers. The bureaucratic paper-pushers, as they were once called, had arrived. But, there were also police, mail carriers, and teachers.

Individuals whose jobs were to handle information eventually outnumbered those who actually made something with their hands. Evolving technology has even shifted the manipulation of data and information largely from clerical to management hands in government offices, like everywhere else. At the same time, clerks who once did nothing more than handle data and information are becoming increasingly responsible for managing data and information, including making decisions about what to do with it. Once, graduating from clerical school meant you were set for a life-long career of typing, filing, and general office duties. Today, digital information processing has made it possible for the same individual to function at a more sophisticated level as well as continuing to type, edit, store, and transmit documents. The nature of executive work has now changed and modem communications technology has made most executives today much more self-sufficient and independent in their work. The magnitude and role of support staff is changing dramatically.

Four-year vs. Life-long Learning

This transformation has changed the concept of learning as a one-time event, be it at university or a trade school, to learning as an ongoing, life-long necessity. Nicholas Imparto of the Hoover Institute at Stanford University says, "It makes sense to regard training more as a process than as a periodic event. In the new economy, learning is an ongoing event and part of everyone's job description as new responsibilities, companies, and industries become the hallmarks of economic development." As long as technological advancement outpaces our mastery of it, as indicated by the growing skills gap, learning will be more and more critical. Life-long learning is vital to the competitiveness of entire organizations and individuals within those organizations. It is the differentiator of the future.

Statisticians have said that if one imagined all of the knowledge gathered by the human race from the beginning of recorded history through 1960 stacked up, the "pile" would be twelve inches high. If one imagines the volume of information and knowledge documented since 1960, the "pile" would be higher than the Washington Monument. This creates an interesting comparison because digital technology and processing, and our ability to access, process, and store knowledge and information, is now far greater than our ability to grasp it. The industrial economic model has yielded to the knowledge/information model, which is yielding to the communications model.

Communication reminds me of the Energizer Bunny: it goes on and on and on. The difficulty of changing corporate culture has been compared to herding cats. The urgency, however, to keep apace with evolving technology is forcing cultural change, vis-à-vis organizational learning, and companies are responding faster and faster. If your organization hasn't yet moved organizational learning up the priority list, it is certain that you are paying for it in decreased productivity, missed opportunities, and lost sales.

The Evolving Economies

The birth of a knowledge economy doesn't mean that industrial manufacturing is obsolete any more than the arrival of the industrial economy brought an end to agriculture. These paradigm shifts represent large trends with many subtrends nesting within them. Let's examine

The Old Industrial Economy	The New Knowledge Economy
Training is a cost center	Training is a competitive advantage
Four-year degree	Life-long learning
Learners travel to school	School travels to the learner
Geographical institutions	Brand name schools w/celebrity professors
Classrooms, correspondence, and video	High-tech interactive multimedia
Standardized training	Customized training
"Just in case" philosophy	"Just in time" philosophy
Limited learning contacts	Virtual learning communities
Learning how to do	Learning how to learn

the industrial vs. knowledge comparisons more closely.

Learning Happens

Formal learning is powerful, tangible, easy to recognize, and to discuss. Informal learning is far more subtle and intangible, but equally as powerful. As management science expert Margaret Wheatley says, "culture happens." In a similar fashion, workplace learning goes on whether you want it to or not. Digital communications and the Internet may have made informal learning far more powerful than formal learning could ever hope to be. The total U.S. budget for formal corporate learning in 2000 exceeded $62 billion. The U.S. budget for all education is about $400 billion dollars. The world resources devoted to education and training exceeds a trillion dollars.

Summary

The Web-based Education Commission, Congressionally sponsored and chaired by Senator Bob Kerrey of Nebraska, has released its report calling for more high-tech training for teachers "Not enough is being done to assure that today's educators have the skills and knowledge needed for effective Web-based teaching." The report urges federal and state support for initiatives that make training and support available to educators.

The commission underlined that the quality of content online varies widely noting, "Dazzling technology has no value unless it supports content that meets the needs of learners." The commission recommends that Congress set content-development priorities and encourage collaboration between the public and private sectors in the distribution of high-quality online materials both in public and corporate education. Accreditation is a voluntary process in which program providers choose to participate. This type of endorsement by academic accreditation bodies helps to validate the quality of programs being offered. New ways of working together must be found.

The commission recommended that the federal government revise the rule requiring that students attend at least twelve hours of course work, half of it in a classroom, in order to be eligible for federal grants or scholarships. Based on that recommendation, the regulation has now changed. This requirement is no longer a major hurdle for students wishing to enroll in online in distance-education courses and is a progressive feature that will move distance learning forward. The e-learning environment will now begin to change.

Another U.S. Department of Education report, *e-*

Learning: Putting a World-class Education at the Fingertips of All Children, outlines five national educational technology goals:

1. All students and teachers must have access to information technology in their classrooms, schools, communities, and homes

2. All teachers must use technology effectively to help students achieve high academic standards

3. All students must have technology and information literacy skills

4. Research and evaluation must improve the next generation of technology applications for teaching and learning, and

5. Digital content and networked applications must transform teaching and learning

I had the privilege of participating on the advisory board of the Web Based Commission that stated, *"In the course of our work we heard from hundreds of educators, policymakers, Internet pioneers, education researchers, and ordinary citizens who shared their powerful visions and showed us the promise of the Internet."* This vision centers on the following precepts:

- *Center learning around the student instead of the classroom*

- *Focus on the strengths and needs of individual learners*

- *Make lifelong learning a practical reality*

- *Apply new knowledge about how people learn, to helping people learn.*

It is in the above context that this chapter has underscored the K–12 imperative for global progress and for individual success, as an imperative for the future workforce development of adults. Casting the 'Net Over Global Learning is central to worldwide success.

*Understanding
changes your
thoughts and
changes your
world.*

—Anonymous

The Way Ahead

We have now examined the four segments of education that form the generic cornerstones of global learning. First, we looked at workforce training and corporate education, including the emerging corporate university, and the new array of chiefs leading the corporate education solutions initiatives and their expansion into new media strategies for workforce training and learning. We have specifically reviewed each segment in the context of e-learning and communications technology. Now it is time to think about their implications for the future. Second, we have explored distance education. Third, we examined adult education, and fourth, the importance of K–12 in establishing the foundation for future success.

There are a number of drivers that we have identified that will make the blended education and e-learning industry one of the most exciting and profitable areas of investment over the next few years. Education and training will make the difference in giving workers and companies an edge in market competition in the near future.

To summarize, K–12 is clearly of key importance in terms of individual success in the future. Higher education, as a major segment of the education establishment, is now embracing workforce training. Adult education that has existed alongside, and overlapping, formal higher education and workforce training, and the emerging corporate university, as a metaphor, is accelerating commercial initiatives in the areas of education and business competition.

Large Industry

The Internet is introducing sweeping change in education and workforce training. The point has been made that the most powerful force revolutionizing education and training is the Internet and the Internet has the capability to quickly and economically transcend international boundaries.

Extracting and atomizing the essential differentiating factors underpinning the trends, I have identified the "silver bullets of e-learning" in the early twenty-first century. They are:

1. Early learning leads to later success

2. The Internet and Web will continue to shrink the world

3. English will dominate as the language of commerce, education, and training

4. Increasing understanding of the physical brain and learning will change learning strategies

5. Theories of specific intelligence will be widely accepted

6. There will be increased understanding of, and respect for, different learning styles

7. Speech will become a principal means of media communications

8. The PC, PDA, and TV will merge

9. Success in interactive media and on-line learning in education and workforce training will proliferate

10. Sensory psychology will develop as a widely recognized knowledge area targeted for study to facilitate in e-learning

11. Semiotics will become an important subject to be studied to prepare for software and technology design

12. The corporate university will become a significant force in world higher education

13. The corporate university will proliferate as an organizational structure for workforce training

14. New career opportunities will continue to expand for chief learning, knowledge, and information executives

15. New masters degree and doctoral degree specialties will increase, providing opportunities for advanced education and research

16. Chief executives in major companies will realize that education and training will give them a competitive edge

17. Print on demand will become common for learning applets and applications.

18. There will be a post-September 11, 2001, paradigm shift from paper to e-communications

19. The Internet and the recordable, Web-connectable DVD will become integrated as tools for learning systems

20. There will be dramatic improvements in screen design, user interface, iconography, and ease of navigation of software

21. Portable, learning-on-the-go applications will become common

22. Technology and high quality sensory programming will shape many markets

23. Personalization in media communications will become better and more common

24. There will be increasing definition and acceptance of new literacies

25. The 'Net will be successfully cast over global learning

Distributed, blended learning solutions will be the way of the future. Partnerships between companies and colleges, and joint programs between colleges and new entities will become common. Organizations have a hard time being good at everything, so companies are choosing areas of development, as well as markets, where they compete. Most customers typically want omnibus solutions. Partnerships generally bring the pieces together for corporate education and training solutions. Combinations of partnerships, therefore, lead to omnibus solutions. This strategy falls into the new field of solutions architecture, which one may think of as the educational counterpart of construction strategies in the construction business.

The demand and acceptance of e-learning is coming from individual company divisions. At this time, the e-learning market is still shaking out.

A big part of the corporate university reach is in training customers. Because of this, speed of response and paralleling customer initiatives that take advantage of the changes have become important. Customizing learning software packages is not all that it appears to be: companies are making choices in structuring learning objects and systems and are using managed outsourcing as a strategy.

Over 84 percent of American four-year colleges offer distance-learning courses, and well over 95 percent of community colleges offer more than 6,000 distance learning courses to an enrollment of more than 2 million students. It is now clear that distance education is far beyond critical mass in America. If the Unites States represents approximately 20 percent of the world's higher education students, simple calculation tells us there are approximately 10 million students enrolled in distance education programs worldwide. (Web-based Education Commission Report, p.77)

Now we must begin to really understand the complexities we face, which and this includes the increasingly diverse populations that must be served. *Intercultural dissonance* is a neglected future dimension. Soon, more than 50 percent of U.S. children in the educational system will be those students who are defined today as minority. In the future, minorities, as we now know them, will be the minority-majority. Now, about one in five K–12 students comes from a household defined as minority, and the same percentage of those kids live in what is defined as poverty. These students are migrating into the workforce in continuing progression. The implications of this situation, while seeming clear as I write this section, are little discussed with respect to either the problem or its solution. The impact of minority-majority population and intercultural dissonance will be part of the problem to be addressed in the United States and certainly permeates the situation faced by global companies and especially Fortune-class companies (as they are all global in today's world). We have a world of worlds. Globalization is not a simple concept. Understanding and sensitivity to multiculturalism is critical.

Academia, governments, and industry are attempting to work together to nurture the Internet's growth, both in terms of distribution and technological advancements. This involves deploying high-performance Internet technologies. What is emerging from these strides is being called "Internet2." Internet2 is represented by a consortium led by over 180 universities in the United States working with more than seventy leading companies to develop and deploy advanced network applications and technologies for research, higher education, and workforce training. This initiative is also called Next Generation Internet (NGI), and will be of major significance.

However it manifests itself, there will be a Next Generation Internet (NGI) and it will include at least two elements:

1. Digital libraries, including HDTV, quality video and CD, quality audio, available on demand. This will avail everyone access to certain previously restricted information.

2. Tele-collaboration, that will enable employees, teachers or students separated by hundreds, and even thousands of miles, to interact with each other as if they were sitting across the table.

Applications enabled by high-performance networking, new work-arounds using new DVD techniques such as *updatability, recordability,* and *connectability,* promise to transform both training and education. Wireless-ness is emerging. It is much cheaper to build cellular relay stations than to lay miles of cable, and wireless solutions will enable underdeveloped and remote areas to quickly partake of the new global Web dimensions via wireless phones, two-way pagers, handheld devices of all types, and the emerging PCTV combinations. These new technologies will be refined by what are termed "adaptive technologies". These include combinations of speech-recognition, gesture-recognition, text-to-speech conversion, language translation, and sensory immersion. These innovations will change the very substance of network-enhanced communication. It will certainly cast the Net over global learning. Desktop, laptop, and appropriate Internet-enabled handheld and even wearable devices are emerging apace, and the number of households with Internet access is increasing. It is difficult to find a company of any size that is not migrating to a distributed, blended technology metaphor. Disturbingly, having visited several major universities recently, I must report that what I found is an amazingly high level of denial.

This academic denial is in the face of the reality that all children born in the last decade have never known the world without the Web.

Additionally security-related issues are helping universities and corporations hasten the development of their distributed learning capacities.

Rapidly declining computer prices are putting those who can afford it online. IDC reports that education is the second most popular computer application for family households. This shows the potential for the Internet to be used in the areas of education and training, including corporate education.

The newest future dimensions of the Internet in training and learning will be recognition, focus, and development of the new learning psychologies. Parts of the emerging knowledge areas related to casting the net over global learning include situational cognition, intercultural dissonance, semiotics, semantics, synesthetics, sensory psychologies, understanding the brain and brain-based learning, new knowledge about systems theory, motivation and learning, positive addiction, and the combined uses of color, graphics, and sound.

Finally, there are the new literacies. For more than twenty years, Professor Howard Gardner of Harvard University, has researched and substantiated the nature of specific intelligence. Gardner provides substantive documentation of eight areas of specific intelligence. They are linguistic, logical-mathematical, intra-personal, inter-personal, spatial, musical, body-kinesthetic, and environmental. I believe that the hypothesis for multiple intelligences applies in the same way to multiple literacies. Most of us tend to be print-centric because of our culture and history in a paper-and-ink world. As the connected audio, visual, and graphics world matures, we will come to recognize multiple literacies in the same way we are now recognizing multiple intelligences.

Multiple intelligence, multiple literacies, new online learning and media psychologies, wired and wireless digital breakthroughs, globalization, and a new energy and spirit of change will help cast the 'Net over global learning. Corporate education and training, K–12, higher, and adult education will never be the same again.

Therefore, we must have a deep understanding of the way ahead. For example, in media and language communications, our programs must do more than focus on reading and the recognition vocabulary. And, when the oral vocabulary is addressed, enunciation and alliteration must be taught in ways that facilitate communication. Cultural dissonance, including issues surrounding first and second language use, are critical subjects. In the western world today, English is the acknowledged language of commerce.

Comprehensive global programs in communication and media are needed to facilitate the concept of the 'Net and global learning. It will allow us to connect ourselves with other peoples, global companies and the world's workforce. The 'Net and global communication means we are obliged to empower *meaning* and improve efforts to work together for a better world.

Shaping global learning includes understanding a number of key trends. In this book we have examined and learned that:

- Everything changes everything
- The emerging corporate university is a significant metaphor for the future
- New chief learning leadership roles are emerging in corporations
- The new psychologies and literacies of global learning are important
- Early learning is important for our workforce of the future
- The new Net will be a web of global learning
- Better communication will bind all people together.

Bibliography

CHAPTER 1

Bagasao, P. Y., Macias, E., Jones, S., Pachon, H. *Challenge to Bridging the Digital Divide: Building Better On-ramps to the Information Highway.* Los Angeles: Tomas Rivera Policy Institute, 1999.

Berst, J. *Tech 2001: The Totally Wired Workforce.* Z.D. Net, 2000. [Electronic Newsletter].[November 23, 2000].

Blumenstyk, G. "Company That Owns the University of Phoenix Plans For a Major Foreign Expansion." *The Chronical of Higher Education* (2000)

Carlson, S. "Psychologists at Towson University Help a Start-up Offer Online Counseling." *The Chronical of Higher Education* (2000)

Carlson, S. "An Ususual Venture at University of Chicago On Open Software." *The Chronical of Higher Education* (2000)

Friedman, T. L. *The Lexus and the Olive Tree.* New York: Farrar, Straus, Giroux, 1999.

Jesdanan, A. "Web Enhances Family Communication." *Associated Press.*

Lotus Development Corporation. *Learning Space 4.0 White Paper.* 2000.

Luskin, B., Drucker, P. "The Coming Change In Our Schools." *AACC Reports* (1981)

Weise, E. "Information Everywhere, But No Time To Think." *U.S.A. Today, Vol.#44* (2000)

CHAPTER 2

Jeanne C. Meister, *Corporate Universities: Lessons in Building a World-class Work Force.* New York: McGraw-Hill/ASTD (1998)

Michael Schrage, *"Campus Clones or Automated Autodidacts?"* Fortune XXI. #(1999)

Danny Cox and John Hoover, *Leadership When the Heat's On.* (New York: McGraw-Hill, 1992).

James W. Michaels, *"Drucker's Disciple."* Forbes Vol. XXI (2000)

The Commission on Technology and Adult Learning: A Joint Project of the American Society for Training and Development (ASTD) and the National Governors' Association (NGA). www.astd.org

Sharon Beder, *"Corporate Universities: For better or worse?"* Engineers Australia, www.uow.edu.au, October 1999.

Webucation. EDUPAGE, May 23, 2000.

Wolensky, Howard, *"Students Crowd E-classrooms."* Howard Wolensky Business Reporter Vol. 17, (2000).

Brandon Hall, Ph.D. *"Special Report on e-Learning."* Forbes Vol. XXI: pg.76.

David Holcombe, "What Drives Corporations to E-learning? www.influent.com, 2000.

Howard Wolinsky: *"Students Crowd E-classrooms."* Howard Wolinsky Business Reporter Vol. 17 (2000)

Mel Duvall, *"E-learning Making the Grade."* Interactive Week Vol. # (2000): pg 46.

Friedman, T. L. *The Lexus and the Olive Tree* (New York: Farrar, Straus, Giroux), 1999.

Michael Schrage, *"Campus Clones or Automated Autodidacts?"* Fortune XXI. #(1999)

Danny Cox and John Hoover, *Leadership When the Heat's On.* (New York: McGraw-Hill, 1992).

James W. Michaels, *"Drucker's Disciple."* Forbes Vol. XXI (2000)

Wolensky, Howard, *"Students Crowd E-classrooms."* Howard Wolensky Business Reporter Vol. 17, (2000).

Brandon Hall, Ph.D. *"Special Report on e-Learning."* Forbes Vol. XXI: pg.76.

Ibid.

David Holcombe, "What Drives Corporations to E-learning? www.influent.com, 2000.

Howard Wolinsky: *"Students Crowd E-classrooms."* Howard Wolinsky Business Reporter Vol. 17 (2000)

Ibid.

Mel Duvall, *"E-learning Making the Grade."* Interactive Week Vol. # (2000): pg 46.

Ibid.

Ibid.

Friedman, T. L. *The Lexus and the Olive Tree* (New York: Farrar, Straus, Giroux), 1999.

CHAPTER 4

Whit Andrews: A New Executive for Net Era: The Chief Knowledge Officer. www.internetworld.com, July 12, 1997

Michael J. Earl & Ian A. Scott: *What is a Chief Knowledge Officer?* In Carolyn Nilson's *Training & Development Yearbook 2000* (Prentice Hall)

Larry G. Willets: The Chief Learning Officer: New Title for New Times. Reengineering Resource Center, May 1996. www.reengineering.com

Diane Frank: GSA Names Remez as Chief Knowledge Officer. Federal Computer Week, June 9, 1999. www.fcw.com

Brian Friel: *GSA Appoints Chief Knowledge Officer.* GovExec.com, June 14, 1999. www.govexec.com

Summary of Survey Results. FCW.com, May 2000.

CSC Names Carol Brothwell Chief Knowledge Officer. News release on December 15, 1999 from www.csc.com

Chief Knowledge Officer Profile. Strategy Software, Inc., 2000. www.strategy-software.com

CHAPTER 5

Ken Freed, "A History of Distance Education: Interactive distance learning at last." Media Visions Webzine.

John Berry, "Traditional Training Fades in Favor of E-learning: Internet economy demands a more flexible training approach." INTERNETWEEK, February 14, 2000.

Elliott Maise in *Capitalizing on e-Learning to Achieve Business Results: A guide to optimizing performance.* SmartForce, 2000.

George Washington University. Distance Learning at The George Washington University. www.gwu.edu, [April 20, 1999].

John Berry, "Traditional Training Fades in Favor of E-learning: Internet economy demands a more flexible training approach." INTERNETWEEK, [February 14, 2000].

Sarah Carr "Challenging Commercial Vendors: George Washington U. enters courseware market." The Chronicle of Higher Education, www.chronicle.com, [April 20, 2000].

"Wiring the Ivory Tower," Business Week, www.businessweek.com, [April,2000].

Glenn C. Altschuller and Ralph Janis, "Promise and Pitfalls in Distance Education for Alumni." The Chronicle of Higher Education, http://chronicle.com.

"Education Anytime, Anywhere: Redefining education." www.trendsreport.net [September 2000].

Webucation. EDUPAGE, , [May 23, 2000].

Amy Westfeldt, "Campus Requires Online Courses." Associated Press, October 17, 2000.

Brandon Hall, "E-learning – Building competitive advantage through people and technology," www.forbes.com.

John Berry, "The E-Learning Factor." Corporate Training June, (2000).

Chris Young, "Founders Learn from aLesson.com." Daily Bruin Online, www.dailybruin.ucla.edu, [June 5, 2000].

Brian Miller, "IBT Financial Adds to its Client list." d.business.com, www.dbusiness.com, [June 7, 2000].

Mavis Scanlon, "L.A.'s E-learning is Booming." Ibid [June 6, 2000].

Howard Wolinsky, "Students Crowd E-classrooms." Newsletter, May 1, 2000.

Scott McNealy, "How to Turn the World Wide Web Into a Real-World Education," Final Edition, (1999)

Mark Walsh, "Online Education: The good, the bad, and the ugly," ECompany Now, June 28, 2000.

Brandon Hall, "E-learning--Building competitive advantage through people and technology," www.forbes.com

CHAPTER 6

Barron, F. The Shaping of Personality: Conflict, Choice, and Growth. New York: Harper & Row Publishers, Inc., 1979.

Caine, R. N., Caine, G. Unleashing the Power of Perceptual Change: The Potential of Brain-based Learning. New York, 1998.

Carter, R., Frith, C. Mapping the Mind. Berkley: University of California Press, 1999.

Coleman, D. P. Emotional Intelligence. New York: McGraw Hill, 2000.

Costa, P. T., II., Widiger, T. A. III. Personality Disorders and the Five Factor Model of Personality (2d ed.). Washington, DC: American Psychological Association, 1994.

Csikszentmihalyi, M. *The Evolving Self: A Psychology for the Third Millenium.* New York: HarperCollins, 1994.

Damasio, A. R. *Descartes' Error: Emotion, Reason and the Human Brain.* New York: Gosset & Dunlap, 1994.

Ellenberger, H. F. *The Discovery of the Unconscious.* New York: Basic Books, 1970.

Ewen, R. B. *Introduction to Theories of Personality* (4th ed.). New Jersey: Lawrence Erlbaum Assoc., Inc, 1993.

Furth, H. G. *Knowledge as Desire.* New York: Columbia University Press, 1987.

Gillham, J. E. *The Science of Optimism and Hope: Research Essays in Honor of Martin E. P. Seligman.* Philladelphia: Temple Foundation Press, 2000.

Glasser, W. *Reality Therapy* (1 ed.) (Vol. 1). New York: Harper Colophon, 1975.

Glasser, W. *Positive Addiction* (2nd ed.) (Vol. 1). New York: Harper Colophon, 1985.

Goleman, D. *Emotional Intelligence.* New York: Bantam Books, 1995.

Hall, C. S. L., G. *Theories of Personality* (3 ed.). New York: Wiley, 1978.

Howard, J. P. *The Owner's Manual for the Brain: Everyday Applications from Mind-Brain Research* (1 ed.) (Vol. 1). Marietta, GA: Bard Press, 2000.

Jensen, E. *Teaching With the Brain in Mind.* Alexandria, VA: Association for Supervision and Curriculum Development, 1998.

Jones, E. *The life and work of Sigmund Freud.* (Vol. 1). New York: Basic Books, 1953.

Kirschner, S., Kirschner, D. A. *Perspectives on Psychology and the Media* (1 ed.) (Vol. 1). Washington, DC: American Psychological Association, 1997.

Kotulak, R. *Inside the Brain* (1st ed.) (Vol. 1). Kansas City: Andrews McMeel Publishing, 1997.

Luskin, T. T., Luskin, B. J. "The History of Media." *Annual Review of Communications: International Engineering Consortium, 53* (Annual Review), (2000)

Luskin, T. T., Luskin, B. J. "Worklife Learning: The New Mantra of .com and .edu." *The Heller Report, 5:7* (January 2000): p. 50.

Maslow, A. H. *Toward a Psychology of Being* (2 ed.). New York: Van Nostrand, 1968.

McConnell, J. "Memory Transfer Through Cannibalism in Planaria." *Journal of Neuro-Psychiatry Vol. VII* (1962):

McCrae, R. R., Costa, P.T. II. "Personality Trait Structure as a Human Universal." *American Psychologist, 52* (May): p. 509 – 516.

Pert, C. B. *Molecules of Emotion: Why You Feel the Way You Feel.* New York: Scribner, 1997.

Pinker, S. *How the Mind Works.* New York: W.W. Norton & Company, Inc, 1997.

Postman, N. *Amusing Ourselves to Death* (1st ed.). New York: Penguin Books, 1985.

Restak, R. *The Brain Has a Mind of Its Own: Insights from a Practicing Neurologist.* New York: Crown Publishing, 1993.

Schacter, D. L. *The Brain, the Mind, and the Past.* New York: Basic Books, 1997

Seligman, M. E. P. *The Optimistic Child* New York:Harper Perennial Library, 1996

Seligman, M. E. P., Csikszentmihaly, C. "Positive Psychology: An Introduction." *American Psychologist, 55* (2000): p. 5 – 14.

Ungar, G. "Scotophbia in Laboratory Rats." *Nature Journal (1972*

Watson, J. D. *The Double Helix* (1st ed.). London: W.W. Norton & Company, Inc, 1980.

Winter, D. G. *Personality: Analysis and Interpretation of Lives.* Boston: McGraw-Hill, 1996.

CHAPTER 7

Gardener, H. *Art, Mind and Brain.* New York: Basic Books, 1982.

Gardener, H. *Frames of Mind.* New York: Basic Books, 1983.

Gardener, H. *Creating Minds.* New York: Basic Books, 1993.

Gardener, H. *Multiple Intelligences: The Theory in Practice.* New York: Basic Books.

Luskin, T. T. *Critical Factors Comprising New Media Literacies for the Early 21st Century Workforce.* Santa Barbara, CA: The Fielding Graduate Institute, Santa Barbara, 2002.

Marks-Tarlow, T. *Creativity Inside Out: Learning Through Multiple Intelligences.* Reading, MA: Addison-Wesley, 1995.

Ruth Palombo Weiss, "Howard Gardner Talks about Technology." www.astd.org, [September, 2000].

Cary Cherniss and Mitchel Adler, *Promoting Emotional Intelligence in Organizations: Making Training in Emotional Intelligence Effective.* (Washington D.C.:ASTD Press, 2000)

CHAPTER 9

www.edgate.com

Jeanne Meister, *Corporate Universities: Lessons in Building a World Class Work Force.* New York:McGraw-Hill/ASTD, (1998), Page 220.

Kian Ghazi, *The Adult Education Market: A comprehensive guide.* Lehman Brothers 1997. (Cited In Jeanne Meister's, *Corporate Universities: Lessons in building a world class work force).*

Jeanne Meister, *Corporate Universities: Lessons in building a world class work force.* McGraw-Hill/ASTD 1998.

Nancy Dillon and Barb Cole-Gomolski: *Depth of IT Skills Shortage Depends on Timing, Training.* ComputerWorld, July 5, 1999.

Howard M. Block, Ph.D. and Lara Izlan, *"Workplace Learning: An introduction to white knights and the skills gap."* Technology Research, (1998)

Michael Kanellos, *"IBM, Intel Chips: Smaller and faster."* ZDNet News, [December 11,2000].

"Teaming Up to Build a Better Worker." Business Week, www.businessweek.com, [August 9, 1999].

Senge, P. *The Fifth Discipline: The Art and Practice of the Learning Organization,* (New York: Currency/Doubleday, 1990): Page 340.

Media, Communication, and the Socio-Psychomedia Effect

By:
Bernard J. Luskin and Toni T. Luskin

SIMPLE TIMES ARE GONE FOREVER

This is the year to review where we have been, to know where we are, and to envision where we want to go. In the context of media and society, a dramatic milestone is reached, for as electricity and the telephone forever changed life at the entrance to the 20th Century, the Internet dramatically alters significant aspects of daily life as we cross the threshold into this 21st Century. Because of the Internet, the world will never be the same again. *Simple times are gone forever…*

PERSPECTIVE

It is now well accepted that mass media have dramatic and continually increasing impact in our lives and behavior. They instill values, both right and wrong, foster aggression and imagination in children, shape the outcomes of elections, encourage both homogenization and dissonance within our cultures and between those to whom we relate. And, the media have a significant impact on the family in many ways. The impact of media on society is the seminal societal subject of the media itself.

We are immersed in media stimuli. Media has become so pervasive and we are so used to the stimuli now, that we are like fish. Fish aren't really conscious of the water… until it isn't there. The term *Socio-Psychomedia Effect* was coined at Luskin International during the course of research conducted for the American Psychological Association, Media Psychology Division, *Task Force Study of Psychology and New Technologies,* in 1997. The study examined the future of new technologies but did not examine the history of media. *The Annual Review of Communications* is an appropriate forum to examine media, communications and their societal effects.

Throughout the 20th century, television, newspapers, books, radio, motion pictures, magazines, recordings, personal computers, CD-ROMs, DVD, satellites, cable and e-mail, all emerged, affecting society as a whole, the family unit and each individual.

In this century the stimuli of mass media became sensory, engendering experiences from what we sense through our senses, i.e., our eyes, ears, nose, and even our skin and our touch. These media stimuli create perceptions that help define what we believe. The gestalt of the effect of media on cultures, families, and individuals may be termed, the Socio-Psychomedia Effect.

In order to thoroughly understand the Socio-Psychomedia Effect in theory and application, it is useful to briefly examine the history and evolution of various 20th century media in the context of the continuously accelerating rate of new developments.

BOOKS

An average of well over 3 million books are sold in the United States every day. And, with book sales now available over the Internet, there is a quantum effect, involving the sale of print books and the birth of e-books. Simultaneous with the growth of television, the popularity of books has continued to grow, not decline, as often predicted previously. In addition, millions of books are checked out from libraries and borrowed from friends so books now circulate as natural elements in our daily lives.

NEWSPAPERS

Until the early part of the nineteenth century, newspapers were quite expensive. A year's subscription cost as much as a skilled laborer could earn in a week. As a result, the majority of the early 20th century public did not read newspapers. Then the "penny press" emerged bringing all economic classes into the ranks of newspaper readers. In 1833, Horace Greeley launched the *New York Morning Post,* followed by the successful *New York Sun,* edited by Benjamin H. Day. Greeley became one of the most famous publishers in the United States. It was the penny press, however, intended for the general public that revolutionized the newspaper business. Greeley sold individual copies instead of subscriptions, speeding up and expanding news coverage and human-interest stories, and including comics to appeal to a wider readership than its predecessors. So, the penny press democratized the newspaper business.

Before 1900, newspapers were intended largely for men, for a variety of social and political reasons. In the early part of this century, however, women became an important literary and political force. In fact, newspapers evolved into a major factor in fostering the spread of print centric literacy. Newspapers have had dramatic impact on the democratization of information and knowledge and in the globalization of ideas.

MAGAZINES

The word magazine comes from an Arabic word meaning "storehouse" or "repository" for goods and merchandise. Just as with newspapers, until the end of the 19th century, magazines were mostly for the elite. During the first half of the 20th century, the magazine became a mass communication medium. Today there are magazines for every conceivable interest, for almost every conceivable type of person, and for every lifestyle and every stage of life. In addition to their social influence, there are thousands of business magazines, professional and trade journals that facilitate a host of special interests.

As one would suspect, surveys show that the magnitude of magazine reading is highly correlated with education. The more educated people are, the more time they are likely to spend reading magazines or journals. Also, magazines that appeal primarily to women outsell magazines that appeal primarily to men.

The effects of magazines have been significant. Women's magazines have helped to shape culinary techniques, health and exercise consciousness, home and office decorating and women's, men's and children's clothing styles. Magazines such as *Playboy, Esquire,* and *G.Q.* have affected the clothing styles, lifestyles, social and sexual attitudes of men and women. Some magazines have become a source for change on many levels. Examples such as *Cosmopolitan* or *Self,* which encourage women to consider new social and professional roles, behaviors and outlooks, are strategically significant in our culture. The *National Review, George,* or *The New Republic,* are examples of magazines that represent a wide range of political ideologies.

Magazines shape the thinking of many of us as we learn and share what our peers around the world are thinking and saying.

MOTION PICTURES

A key step in the development of "moving" pictures emerged from an understanding of how our eyes perceive motion. This phenomenon was first reported by an English physician, Peter Mark Roget, in a scientific paper "The Persistence of Vision With Regard to Moving Objects." Roget discovered that our eyes retain an image for a fraction of a second after each object we are looking at disappears. This is called "after image." This explains, in part, why we can sometimes continue to see images on our television screens after switching our televisions off. Roget put the idea to use in a book of pictures you (the reader) can rapidly flip through thereby creating the mental image of motion. Motion pictures, that are simply a series of pictures projected in rapid succession (24 frames per second for basic full motion) carried Roget's idea, spawning movies as the tremendous social force we know today.

It was not until recent years, however, that the concepts of multiple intelligences and new media literacies began to emerge. In the 1980's technological developments and consumer demand began to blur the distinction between the motion picture and video industries. The coming of the VCR did not adversely impact movie theater attendance and it expanded the motion picture market capture to include the sale and rental of films. Now, advertiser support for movies on commercial TV networks, subscription networks and pay-per-view abound. The motion picture industry changed dramatically in the late 20s, early 50s, and in the 80s by the addition of new technological breakthroughs. And movies continue to significantly affect the way we live. In the 80s, with the advent of home VCRs for example, movie theater attendance went up, compounded by huge growth in the sale and rental of videocassettes. The visual image, both still and moving, is a permeating social force. Each emerging new media format seems to have its own following, that in turn, seems to stimulates other formats.

RECORDINGS

No mass medium mirrors the thoughts and *feelings* of our generation more than recorded music. The social dun of war, drugs, sexual freedom and its consequences, the continuing erosion of the nuclear family, growing communication, and the integration and alienation of many minorities, echo globally in recorded music. Recorded music provides a broad range of entertainment, information, persuasion, and influence. Recordings of poetry, drama, oral history, comedy, religious and political sermons, and educational articulations all have significant influence on individuals, the family and society.

The record industry continues to boom. All major record companies are now part of larger communications conglomerates and the "majors" control 95% of the record business. Warner, Universal, and Sony Records dominate the American and world record business.

Music as well as books, newspapers, magazines, motion pictures, and television have always been, and continue to be, used for persuasive purposes. They sell soap and beer. They drum ideas and sell political candidates. All these media stimulate society and bring about social change, having staggering impact on our families and on our personal values.

As examples of the societal effects of ever-present musical recordings on our perception and behavior, we need only observe how music in the 1980s embraced drugs or how music in the 1970s addressed the war in Vietnam. Messages sent by the media are continually being absorbed by our consciousness. The common music of each generation has also given each generation a set of early common, and later cherished, experiences. Music gives us memories and also gives a sense of community to each generation.

Now, digital recordings, recordable Cds, and other playback techniques are revolutionizing recorded sound both technically and socially. Our music and recordings affect all aspects of our lives. Politics, religion, the values of our country, our means of stimulating or protesting war, racial discrimination, working conditions, laws and mores are all the stuff of the music of the generations. How dramatically different our lives would be without "the sound of music."

RADIO

Radio must also be examined in the context of "most important" advances in mass communication. While music represents the message, radio represents the massage. It extended the reach and the democratization of communication throughout the world for the first time. Print requires an audience to read. Radio is a medium that demands no special skill from its audience. For this reason, radio has become a powerful medium for educational and propaganda purposes in all underdeveloped parts of the world, even today, and for information and entertainment everywhere.

Radio follows us. Its sounds fly through the air. Portable radios and car radios are socially pervasive. The average household in America has a half dozen radio receivers and 95% of the world's cars have radios. While the average American may not be consciously aware, he or she spends at least several hours each day with a radio. The overt and subliminal influences of radio bombard joggers, rollerbladers, sports enthusiasts at events, people in their cars, in elevators, callers "holding" on the telephone, and people walking on the streets. Almost all people have radios and the reach and effect of radio permeates all but a very few places on earth.

In addition, the telegraph and the telephone are both radio's cousins. During the latter part of the 19th century, the telephone was neither conceived nor perceived as being the tool for mass communication it is today. Ironically, its inventor, Alexander Graham Bell, naively voiced his dream and goal that someday there would be *a telephone* in every major city.

World War I actually spurred the development of radio. The armed forces needed a dependable means of communication so the technical aspects and global use of radio were spurred to advance. Interestingly, just before World War I, educational radio stations were already operating in Nebraska, North Dakota, and Wisconsin. This was because early broadcasts were designed to serve farmers in rural America with important weather and market reports and news highlights. The University of Wisconsin radio station was the first officially licensed station in 1914 and marks the agrarian's stimulus for radio.

Just as horseless carriages begat automobiles, the marriage of radio to *the flickers* begat *radio pictures,* which begat motion pictures with *sound,* and they in turn spawned television and much of it's programming. Radio held a dominant societal/communications place during World War II. Listening was more planned 60 years ago. Listening today is largely unplanned. Now, many people wake with radio, go to sleep with radio, and listen during morning and evening rush hour commutes. Radio stimulates the imagination and allows people to use their imaginations to form visual images from the sounds they hear. Radio represents a world that exists in the mind and some of the most vivid pictures one can see are produced in our minds by the stimulus of radio. Psychovisualization is one phenomena of radio listening. Radio is a superb exercise medium for the imagination.

Although most of us do not realize it, in story telling, the sound of a word can be as important as it's meaning. Great dramatic actors, such as Sir Lawrence Olivier, Richard Burton, and Orson Wells understood this. They were renowned for practicing and vocalizing to make the perfect tones and emphasis on words to achieve the desired effects upon a listening audience.

Radio is a source of both reality and fantasy. At the broadcaster's will, we may be switched back and forth between fact and fiction. Advertisers have learned to manipulate these phenomena with great effect on consumers.

Every medium of mass communication goes through a series of stages in its development to maturity and that is still true of radio, which interestingly, is having a new 21st century digital boom.

TELEVISION

Television has transformed life in the developed world. It has changed the daily habits of people. It has both molded and memorialized the style of each generation of viewers. Television makes immediate global phenomena out of local happenings. Television, now via satellite transmission, transforms and channels events and information into "hot" live programming accessed in nearly every home. Television has profoundly affected the social process and the ways in which people behave everywhere in the world.

Through television we see violence and sexual contact, we respond to stereotypical portrayals of populations within populations. We view banal programming and observe politicians as they joust with their issues. With nearly 100% penetration throughout the world, there is hardly a home without a television set. In fact, there are more television sets in the United States than bathtubs. On that fact we shall make no further comment.

The major spurt in the development of television technology was during and following World War II. Cable systems, communication satellites and microwave relays each now facilitate the delivery of television programs to the home. We have more and more channels and more and more programming aimed at us. Reality and the art of fantasy are confused in television. Yet, television is now an integral and indispensable part of our lives. Television provides common ways of perceiving a common base of information. It gives us a means to share experiences and sets a ceaseless flow of electronic stimuli streaming into our living, family and bedrooms.

Some groups and individuals have gone to extreme lengths to gain access to the world's television audience. Terrorists, for example, have hijacked airliners and taken hostages in front of global audiences. The Ayatollah Kohmanie (Iran), Sadam Hussein (Iraq), Mohamar Kadaffe (Libya), Tienamin Square (China), Berlin Wall (dismantling USSR) are all recent examples of political crisis played out on a stage of international television coverage. Because of television, English has become the universal language of news, commerce, and protest. The effects of television are universal.

COMPUTERS

The personal computer has also become an integral part of mass communication. Videotext and teletext are ways of bringing specialized print information to the home via the television set or personal computer. Concepts pioneered in videotext or teletext, are seeing new e-book and pocketbook incarnations. And, the computer and the television set *are* merging. The TVPC and PCTV now represent differences without a distinction, except for the designer features determining how each of these delivery systems will look based on where they will be set within the home. Convergence is a 21st century phenomenon.

SATELLITES

Satellites have had enormous impact on recent mass communication. Satellites have made instantaneous transmission of pictures, sound and data a reality. Key satellites circle the earth in stationary "geosynchronous" orbit, their paths synchronized with the rotation of the earth. A satellite receives signals from an "uplink," or transmitting station on the ground. It amplifies the signals and relays them back to the ground in the form of a "footprint" by means of a set of transponders, i.e., small transmitters, aboard. The signals go back to different earth locations that the space located satellite can see on the ground, including cable systems, television stations and other "downlinks," for distribution. The footprint of a satellite signal may be confined to a small area or may cover a whole continent.

New systems such as direct-broadcast satellites (DBS) send signals directly into home to television receivers and small home satellite dishes. Two-way cable is another emerging dimension of this technology and interactive cable is now evolving through both the television set and the PC. PC-ROM and TV-RAM are becoming common vernacular of the day. Wireless cable is another emerging technology so the future will see both wired and wireless innovations. Low power television (LPTV), high definition television (HDTV), microchip advances and miniaturization all continue to push the evolving technological, communications envelope. The simplest way to think about these concepts for the purposes of this paper is that all programming is now either broadcast or non-broadcast, wired or wireless. I am speaking only of technologies in place today. Digital wired and wireless formats will abound in the coming years.

WORLD WIDE WEB AND THE INTERNET

Net surfing and webcasting leads to two-way communication between PCs all over the world. The numbers of people setting up chat rooms and participating in on-line discussions are increasing at a rapid rate. When TV-type programming on a PC or, PC-type programming on a TV is further perfected, more dramatic changes will occur.

The use and abuse of e-mail is booming. E-mail is proving very effective for efficient communication on professional, commercial and personal levels. E-mailboxes, however, are presently being over run by advertisers and senders of junk e-mail, and because of this there is some *weblash* from the collision of good messages with junk e-mail. The present explosion of junk e-mail also worries privacy advocates. New times and new technologies mean new rules. Furor over the deluge of unwanted electronic mail ignites the emotional participation of vast numbers of individuals, often creating a further deluge. However, all of the bandwidth limitations are disappearing.

All of the media discussed have an impact on society, the family, the future of media and social psychology, as we strive to understand and deal with the relationship between media and the self.

The social impact of mass media communication continues to increase as the population also increases. The actual number of households in the United States is increasing significantly because of the increasing number of people who choose to live alone. Our suburbs continue to grow at the expense of our large, urban cities. More than half the adult women in the United States now have full time jobs. More than 60% of all mothers with children under 5 years of age, work fulltime. People are changing professions and occupations more frequently. The US Department of Labor says that people in the 21st century are likely to change jobs an average of 10 times during their working years. Greatly enhanced communication technologies will accelerate changes through their almost immediate and widespread transmission of images of any new lifestyle, thus shortening the potential "adoption" and "adaptation" time for changing values. Online delivery systems for corporate workforce training in America will facilitate the professional growth and changes necessary for early 21st century employment.

The nature of work-education is changing. Also, as more women enter the workforce, we see a breakdown of traditional inter-personal relationships because of increased blurring of traditional role separations previously occurring between male and female roles in the home. 21st century workforce changes and increased education and opportunity for women will continue to cause specific changes such as the sharing of homemaking tasks, like cooking, caring for children, cleaning, and shopping for household goods. Interestingly, these role shifts will strikingly impact advertising currently designed to appeal to housewives, but which will need to be redesigned to accommodate the interests and needs of both genders.

Because of the changing nature of work, personal growth drives, changing jobs, and increased accessibility, the demand for education, retraining and re-specialization will now increase at warp speed. This has implications for the use of all media in learning in the traditional institutions and, certainly, in the burgeoning distance learning environment, as well as the new and growing phenomena of the corporate university which is growing apace. At this writing, more than 2,000 corporate universities of all types have been announced and the number is increasing rapidly.

SOCIO-PSYCHOMEDIA EFFECT: "What a tangled web we weave…"

Those who understand the media psychology of producing newspapers, magazines, books, movies, recordings, radio, television, CD-ROMs, Websites, and Internet-based interactive communication, will have major impact on the shape of our future lives. The majority of the populations in developed countries are now comfortable with modern media and the effects of those modern media upon our lives are becoming part of their consciousness.

The immanent, great increase in communications channels made possible by VCRs, cable, fiber optics, satellites, computers, CD-ROMs, Digital Video-ROMs, Internet, and World Wide Web communications will have continuing great social implications.

Where the media begins to serve as a substitute for social interaction, where it has a role in relaxation, diversion, enjoyment, and stimulation, it will also surely affect our social structure and the way we live. Without question, media affects the individuals, families, and society, their self-images and concepts and behaviors, their beliefs about the world and politics, government and religion, education, business, and industry. Constant examination of all of these social elements will continue to spin the World Wide Web and the recognition of *The New Media Literacies* will emerge.

"The Internet changes everything" is the theme of much current literature. All of the media now converge and the Internet of the future will be a combination of each of them, including all forms of wired and wireless communication. The affective and cognitive impact of media on the senses, infrastructure, institutions and digital domains of the early 21st century world are embodied in the concepts that we call, the Socio-Psychomedia Effect. This is best understood within its historical context, including the differences between media effects upon populations of the 20th and the early 21st centuries and the recognition of *Pscybermedia*.

Dr. Toni Thomas Luskin is vice president of Luskin International, a media consulting and production company. She holds a Ph.D. in media studies from The Fielding Graduate Institute. Ms. Luskin is a veteran stage, media and television performer and producer of such series as *"You Asked For It"*, numerous commercials and infomercials, was a lead performer in the famed *Lido de Paris*, and is a specialist in all forms of post-production relating to narration and effect sound. She has written extensively for network, cable and syndicated television. A commercial pilot, Ms. Luskin was the "Eye-In-The-Sky" reporter, flying the airplane and reporting traffic, weather and news.

Reference: Luskin Bernard J., Luskin, Toni T., Annual Review of Communications, Volume 53,International Engineering Consortium, Executive Perspectives, Chicago, Ill, pp.668-672,

Authors Note: several minor changes were made in the article to update it, and also since it was written, we have experienced the traumatic events of 9/11/2001. However, the authors feel that the accuracy is intact and the content is relevant, so it is included here in its entirety.

About the Author

In education, Bernie Luskin was president of Orange Coast College, founding president of Coastline Community College, launched with the largest opening enrollment of any college up to that time. He is a founding executive of KOCE-TV, the Orange County PBS station operated by the Coast Community College District. Dr. Luskin was also founding chancellor of Jones International University; the first fully accredited totally web-based university. Luskin served for nine years on the board of directors of the American Association of Community Colleges, was Chairman, and served in Washington, D.C. as Executive Vice President and COO. He was intimately involved in the original establishment of the Adult Learning Service of PBS. In addition to present service as faculty, EVP for partnerships, and Director of Media Studies and Community College Leadership programs at The Fielding Graduate Institute, he is also Visiting Professor at Claremont Graduate University. He has taught at UCLA, USC, Pepperdine University and various branches of California State University. Luskin has also served as chairman of The National Council for Resource Development, a major association for executives active in capitol formation for non-profit organizations and where he has been recognized for special achievement in the development of public policy and education programs.

In corporate life, Bernie Luskin has served as CEO/president of major divisions of Fortune 50 and 500 companies. Luskin is founding president and CEO of Polygram's American Interactive Media, Philips Interactive Media and Philips Media Education and Reference

Publishing. As CEO of Jones Interactive, Inc., Luskin was also group president of companies which included cable networks, film and television production, education, and telecommunications companies. Several of these companies were Jones Digital Century, Jones Education Networks, including the following television, cable and satellite networks: Jones Computer Network, Knowledge TV, Mind Extension University, The Internet Channel and Jones Management Information Systems. Luskin is founding President and Co-CEO of Global Learning Systems. Presently, Luskin is Chairman and CEO of Luskin International, and as noted earlier, Director of the Media Studies and Community College Leadership programs at the Fielding Graduate Institute.

In media, Dr. Luskin pioneered early programs in compact disc, telecommunications and cable network development. Luskin put the first computer in a community college, wrote the first high school data processing textbook, authored eight best-seller economics, technology and education books, hundreds of articles, directed the research study and produced the model for the television courses presently used in distance learning and which served as the basis for legislation enabling state funds to be used for non-classroom based instruction, opening the way for independent study and distance education. Luskin has produced many television programs and series, which have received significant recognition. He has also produced many CD-Rom and DVD programs and learning systems, and has constructed agreements establishing major milestones in intellectual property. Among his many television and CD projects are the first Sesame Street CD, Treasures of the Smithsonian, Charlton Heston Presents the Bible, Compton's Encyclopedia, Grolier's Encyclopedia, and Voyeur, the first interactive CD movie, starring Robert Culp. Telecourses include The Growing Years, Understanding Psychology, Freehand Sketch, and many others.

While CEO of the new business division of Polygram Records, Luskin led the research initiative to develop the specifications, software and chips, and was a principal in the first deal between Philips and Paramount Studios to digitize motion pictures on compact disc in MPEG format, leading to DVD. He researched, planned and launched the first US compressed cable network. As a learning psychologist, his research specialty is media studies, with a principle emphasis on elearning psychologies. In 1998, he completed a major study of psychology and new technologies for the American Psychological Association, Media Psychology Division (46), defining new uses of media in the fields of learning, commerce, government, medicine and psychology

Dr. Luskin has, or is now serving on the Board of Directors of Polygram Pictures, the California School of Professional Psychology, The Center for the Partially Sighted, the Transportation Foundation of Los Angeles, KLCS TV, High Tech High L.A., Digital Directions International, operating the Private Lessons Channel with PBS Stations and AOL, Creative Frontier, Inc and Imerge, Inc., a leading digital music developer based in the U.K. He is a member of the Board of Visitors in Education at Claremont Graduate University and served on the Accrediting Commission for Collegiate Schools of Business and supervised the production of the media training materials for the Western Association of Schools and Colleges. He presently serves on the Education Policy Committee of The Academy of Television Arts and Sciences, the Millennium Council of the American Film Institute, as a Founder of the L.A. Opera, and the new Los Angeles, Center for the Dance. Luskin regularly serves as Contributing Editor and is a twenty-five year editorial board member of THE Journal. Luskin was appointed by Congress to serve on the National Science Foundation, Science Education Committee. He was appointed by California's governor as a commissioner on the California Postsecondary Education Commission, the oversight body for all California higher education and served as chairman of the program committee, with oversight responsibility for all statewide higher education programs. Luskin also served as evaluator of the New Media Literacy Project conducted by the University of Southern California, Annenberg School of Communication. He is presently active in Empower America, a public policy organization whose co-directors are Bill Bennett, Jack Kemp, Bill Cohen and Jean Kirkpatrick.

With degrees in Business (accounting and management), a license in Family Therapy, and a UCLA doctorate in Technology and Higher Education, Luskin was a UCLA, Kellogg and University Fellow. He is recipient of the UCLA Doctoral Alumni Association, University of Florida, Council for Resource Development, California State University, L.A., and Long Beach City College, awards for leadership in higher education. The European Commission and Irish Government recognized him with lifetime achievement awards for seminal contributions in research and distinguished leadership in digital media.

Bernie Luskin is married to Toni Thomas Luskin and has two sons, Ryan and Matteo.